Nurturing Success
A Teachers Guide to
Supporting Dyslexic
Learners

Garry Anderson

ISBN: 9798852282323

This book is dedicated to my loving family and supportive colleagues who have been unwavering pillars of encouragement and understanding throughout my journey of supporting dyslexic learners. Your belief in my work, your patience, and your unwavering support have been invaluable.

Table of Contents

Foreword

It is with great pleasure and anticipation that I write the foreword for this comprehensive guide to supporting dyslexic learners. As an advocate for inclusive education and a firm believer in the potential of every learner, I am thrilled to see a resource that provides educators with the knowledge, strategies, and tools to create an inclusive learning environment where dyslexic learners can thrive.

Dyslexia, a neurodiverse condition, presents unique challenges in the realm of learning, particularly in areas such as reading, writing, and numeracy. However, it is crucial to recognise that dyslexia does not define the capabilities or potential of individuals. With the right support, dyslexic learners can overcome obstacles, develop their strengths, and achieve academic success.

This book goes beyond just understanding dyslexia; it offers a road map for educators to support dyslexic learners effectively. From dispelling misconceptions and providing an overview of dyslexia to offering practical strategies for differentiated instruction, assistive technology, social-emotional well-being, collaboration with specialists, and more, this guide covers a wide range of essential topics.

One aspect that particularly resonates with me is the emphasis on fostering a dyslexia-friendly classroom environment. Creating a supportive and inclusive space where dyslexic learners feel valued, understood, and empowered is crucial to their overall well-being and success. By implementing the strategies presented in this book, educators can transform their classrooms into inclusive learning communities that embrace the strengths and diversity of all learners.

1

Furthermore, the collaborative approach advocated in this book is commendable. Recognising that dyslexia support requires the collective efforts of educators, specialists, parents, and support services, this guide highlights the importance of collaborative partnerships. By working together and sharing expertise, we can create a comprehensive support system that meets the unique needs of dyslexic learners and promotes their growth and development.

I commend the authors for their meticulous research, comprehensive content, and practical approach to supporting dyslexic learners. Their expertise and passion shine through, making this book an invaluable resource for educators seeking to make a positive difference in the lives of dyslexic learners.

To all educators, specialists, and professionals dedicated to supporting dyslexic learners, I encourage you to embrace the knowledge and strategies presented in this book. Your commitment and advocacy are integral to creating inclusive educational environments where dyslexic learners can reach their full potential.

Together, let us embark on this journey of support, empowerment, and inclusivity. By equipping ourselves with the knowledge and tools to support dyslexic learners, we can create a future where every learner has the opportunity to thrive and succeed.

Garry Anderson

CHAPTER ONE
Introduction

Understanding Dyslexia - Defining Dyslexia

Before we can delve into the big wide world of dyslexia support, we first need to understand what dyslexia is. There is no one universally accepted definition of dyslexia. The British Dyslexia Association (BDA) defines dyslexia as:

"... a specific learning difficulty that primarily affects the skills involved in accurate and fluent word reading and spelling. Characteristic features of dyslexia are difficulties in phonological awareness, verbal memory, and verbal processing speed. Dyslexia occurs across a range of intellectual abilities. It is best thought of as a continuum, not a distinct category, and there are no clear cut-off points."

The NHS defines dyslexia as:

"... a common learning difficulty that can cause problems with reading, writing, and spelling. It's a specific learning difficulty, which means it causes problems with certain abilities used for learning, such as reading and writing. Unlike a learning disability, intelligence isn't affected."

These are just two examples of definitions of dyslexia, and they are both different. Any organisations have their own definitions; however, each definition has common themes throughout them. These common themes are:

1. **Dyslexia is a Specific Learning Difficulty:**

Dyslexia is consistently described as a specific learning difficulty that primarily affects certain skills, such as accurate and fluent word reading, spelling, and phonological awareness.

2. **Challenges in Reading and Writing:**

All definitions emphasise the difficulties dyslexic individuals face in reading, writing, and spelling. This includes struggles with decoding words, reading fluency, comprehension, spelling accuracy, and written expressions.

3. **Phonological Processing Difficulties:**

Definitions commonly mention difficulties in phonological awareness, which refers to the ability to identify and manipulate the individual sounds (phonemes) in spoken language. Phonological processing challenges are often seen as a core characteristic of dyslexia.

4. **Variability Across Intellectual Abilities:**

Dyslexia is recognised as occurring across the range of intellectual abilities. It is not dependent on intelligence and can affect individuals with average or above-average intellectual capabilities.

5. **Lifelong Condition:**

Dyslexia is consistently described as a lifelong condition that persists into adulthood. It is emphasised that although dyslexia cannot be cured, it can be managed and accommodated effectively with appropriate support.

6. **Continuum and Individual Differences:**

Definitions highlight those with dyslexia is best understood as a continuum, not a distinct category. There is no clear-cut off points, and dyslexic individuals exhibit a range of abilities, strengths, and challenges. Everyone with dyslexia is unique and may require personalised support and accommodations.

While the specific wording and emphasis may vary slightly, these common themes reflect the fundamental understanding of dyslexia across various reputable sources and highlight the core characteristics and challenges associated with the condition.

Characteristics of Dyslexia

As mentioned previously, dyslexia is a specific learning difficulty that is characterised by various challenges in reading, writing, and spelling. While the specific characteristics and severity of dyslexia can vary from individual to individual, here are some common characteristics associated with dyslexia:

1. **Reading Difficulties**

Dyslexic individuals often struggle with reading skills, including decoding words, recognising sight words, and achieving reading fluency. They may have difficulty with accurate and efficient word recognition.

2. **Phonological Awareness**

Dyslexia is often marked by difficulties in phonological processing, which refers to the ability to identify and manipulate the individual sounds (phonemes) in spoken language. Dyslexic individuals may have trouble breaking words down into sounds or blending sounds to form words.

3. **Spelling Difficulties**

Dyslexic individuals may exhibit challenges in spelling. They may struggle with phonetic spelling and have difficulty remembering and applying spelling patterns and rules.

4. **Writing Challenges**

Dyslexia can also impact written expression. Dyslexic individuals may find it challenging to organise their thoughts, use appropriate grammar and syntax, and express their ideas coherently in writing.

5. **Slow Reading Rate**

Dyslexic individuals often read at a slower pace compared to their peers. They may require additional time to process and comprehend written text.

6. Working Memory and Processing Speed

Dyslexia may be associated with weaknesses in working memory, which can affect the ability to retain and manipulate information temporarily. Additionally, dyslexic individuals may exhibit slower processing speed, which can impact their ability to complete reading and writing tasks efficiently.

7. Oral Language Skills

While dyslexia primarily affects reading and writing, some individuals may also experience challenges in oral language skills, such as verbal expression, vocabulary acquisition, and understanding complex sentences.

It's important to note that dyslexia is a complex condition, and not all individuals with dyslexia will exhibit the same set of characteristics or experience them to the same degree. The specific combination and severity of characteristics can vary widely, making each dyslexic individual unique. A comprehensive assessment by qualified professionals can help identify and understand the specific profile of strengths and challenges for an individual with dyslexia. However, this is not always necessary, and a profile can be put together by a teacher (this is explained in Chapter 1).

Major Theories of Dyslexia

I won't go into too much detail on the many theories of dyslexia; however, they are worth exploring.

There are several major theories that aim to explain the underlying causes and mechanisms of dyslexia. While the precise causes of dyslexia are still being investigated, these are some prominent theories:

1. Phonological Deficit Theory

This theory suggests that dyslexia is primarily caused by difficulties in phonological processing. Individuals with dyslexia may struggle with accurately recognising and manipulating the sounds of language (phonemes), leading to difficulties in mapping sounds to letters and words during reading and spelling.

2. Visual Processing Deficit Theory

According to this theory, dyslexia is attributed to visual processing difficulties. It suggests that dyslexic individuals have challenges in perceiving and processing visual stimuli related to reading, such as letters, words, and text. Difficulties in visual attention, tracking, and discrimination may contribute to reading difficulties.

3. Cognitive Processing Deficit Theory

This theory suggests that dyslexia is associated with broader cognitive processing deficits, beyond phonological or visual processing. These deficits may include difficulties in working memory, processing speed, attention, and executive functions, which can impact various aspects of reading and writing.

4. Genetic and Neurobiological Theories

These theories focus on the genetic and neurobiological factors underlying dyslexia. Research has identified potential genetic variations that may increase the risk of dyslexia. Neurobiological studies have revealed differences in brain structure and activation patterns in individuals with dyslexia, particularly in areas involved in reading and language processing.

5. Double-Deficit Hypothesis

The double-deficit hypothesis proposes that dyslexia arises from both phonological processing deficits and the rapid automatised naming (RAN) deficits. RAN refers to the ability to quickly name a series of familiar stimuli (e.g., letters, colours, objects). The theory suggests that the co-occurrence of these two deficits exacerbates reading difficulties in dyslexic individuals.

It's important to note that these theories are not mutually exclusive, and dyslexia is likely influenced by a combination of multiple factors. Researchers continue to investigate these theories and explore their interrelationships to deepen our understanding of dyslexia and inform effective interventions and support strategies.

Statistical Overview

Dyslexia is a common learning difficulty worldwide, with prevalence rate varying across studies and populations. According to the British Dyslexia Association (BDA), it is estimated that around 10% of the population has dyslexia. The U.S. National Institute of Health (NIH) suggests that dyslexia affects about 5-10% of the population.

Research has suggested that dyslexia is more commonly diagnosed in males than females, with a male-to-female ratio ranging from 2:1 to 3:1 (Shaywitz et al., 1995; Ziegler et al., 2008).

Dyslexia often co-occurs with other learning difficulties and conditions. Some common overlapping conditions include:

- **Attention-Deficit/Hyperactivity Disorder (ADHD):** Studies have found a higher prevalence of ADHD symptoms among dyslexic individuals compared to the general population (Willcutt et al., 2010).
- **Specific Language Impairment (SLI):** There is an overlap between dyslexia and SLI, with a significant proportion of individuals with dyslexia also experiencing language impairments (Catts et al., 2005).
- **Developmental Coordination Disorder (DCD):** Dyslexia and DCD often co-occur, with motor coordination difficulties frequently observed in dyslexic individuals (Fawcett & Nicolson, 1994).

Dyslexia can have significant implications for academic achievement and long-term outcomes. Research has shown that dyslexic individuals may have lower literacy levels, reduced educational attainment, and increased risk of educational and occupational underachievement (Snowling, 2013).

These statistics provide a general overview of the prevalence, gender differences, comorbidity, and academic outcomes associated with dyslexia. It is important to note that prevalence rates and specific findings may vary across studies and populations.

The Academic Impact of Dyslexia

In this section, we will explore the academic challenges and impact of dyslexia on dyslexic pupils in the classroom. Dyslexia poses significant obstacles to reading, writing, spelling, and numeracy skills. Understanding these challenges is crucial for educators and professionals involved in supporting dyslexic students effectively.

Reading Difficulties

We will begin by delving into reading difficulties experienced by dyslexic pupils. Decoding and word recognition challenges, as well as difficulties in reading comprehension, can hinder their abilities to access and understand written text (Shaywitz & Shaywitz, 2008). Nation & Snowling (2004) go onto the support that comprehension and extracting meaning from written text can also be a challenge for dyslexic pupils, affecting their overall understanding. This can go onto to impact over curricular areas such as science and social studies, where reading comprehension and vocabulary play a crucial role (Jiménez, et al., 2018).

Writing and Spelling Challenges

Spelling accuracy and phonetic spelling issues can impact on dyslexic learners written expression, while struggles with organisation and coherence can affect their clarity of their writing. Furthermore, dyslexia can impact vocabulary acquisition and grammatical skills, affecting their ability to express ideas precisely. Critten et al. (2017) state that dyslexic students often experience difficulties in spelling, relying on phonetic strategies that may result in inaccuracies. Graham & Harris (2005) describe that the organisational thoughts and ideas in written form can be challenging for dyslexic learners, affecting their coherence and clarity in writing. Dyslexia can also impact vocabulary acquisition and grammatical skills, leading to challenges in expressing ideas precisely (Nippold et al., 2005).

Mathematics and Numeracy Difficulties

Dyslexia can also have an impact on mathematical and numeracy skills. Moll et al. (2016) stated that dyslexic pupils may struggle with number identification, sequencing, and memorisation, which affects their mathematical understanding. Dyslexia can make it challenging to understand and solve word problems that involve reading and interpreting mathematical information (Geary, 2004). Dyslexic pupils may also experience difficulties with mathematical reasoning and accurate computation, impacting their overall mathematical performance (Dowker, 2005).

The Emotional and Social Impact of Dyslexia

Dyslexia not only presents academic challenges but can also have significant emotional and social implications for dyslexic pupils. In this section, we will explore the emotional and social impact of dyslexia, examining the difficulties faced by these students and highlighting the importance of fostering a supportive and inclusive environment.

Emotional Challenges

Dyslexic pupils may experience a range of emotional challenges due to their struggles with reading, writing, and spelling. These challenges can include:

- **Frustration and Anxiety:** Difficulties in academic tasks may lead to frustration and anxiety as dyslexic pupils try to keep up with their peers (Sideridis et al., 2006).
- **Low Self-Esteem:** Academic difficulties can impact self-esteem and confidence, as dyslexic pupils may feel inadequate or compare themselves unfavourably to their peers (Pumfrey & Reason, 2001).
- **Feelings of Isolation:** Dyslexic pupils may feel isolated or different from their peers due to their struggles in the classroom (Alexander-Passe, 2006).

Social Implications

Dyslexia can also have social implications for dyslexic pupils, affecting their interactions and relationships with peers. Some common challenges include:

- **Peer Teasing and Bullying:** Dyslexic pupils may become targets of teasing or bullying related to their reading or writing difficulties, which can further impact their self-esteem and social integration (Humphrey & Mullins, 2002).

- **Peer Acceptance:** Difficulties in academic tasks can sometimes hinder dyslexic pupils' social acceptance and their ability to fit in with their peer group (Cillessen & Bellmore, 2011).
- **Limited Participation:** Dyslexic pupils may avoid participating in activities that require reading or writing skills, leading to decreased involvement in social and extracurricular activities (McCoach et al., 2006).

It is crucial for educators and school communities to address the emotional and social impact of dyslexia to support the well-being and social inclusion of dyslexic pupils. By fostering a supportive and inclusive environment, educators can help dyslexic pupils develop resilience, self-advocacy, and positive social interactions.

By addressing the emotional and social impact of dyslexia, educators can create a supportive environment that nurtures the well-being and social integration of dyslexic pupils, promoting their overall development and success.

The Importance of Teacher Support

Effective teacher support plays a crucial role in promoting the success and well-being of pupils with dyslexia. In this section, we will explore the significance of teacher support and it's impact on the academic, emotional, and social development of dyslexic pupils. Emphasising the importance of a collaborative and inclusive approach, we will highlight strategies and practices that can empower teachers to effectively support their dyslexic students.

Building Rapport and Trust

Establishing a positive and trusting relationship with dyslexic pupils is essential. Teachers can create a supportive environment by demonstrating empathy, patience, and understanding (MacArthur et al., 2016). Building rapport helps to foster a sense of safety and belonging, which can enhance engagement and self-confidence.

Individualised Instruction and Differentiated Learning

Providing individualised instruction that addresses the specific needs of dyslexic pupils is crucial. Differentiated learning plans, tailored to their strengths and challenges, enable teachers to offer targeted support (Pemberton & Watkins, 2012). This may involve implementing multisensory teaching techniques, incorporating assistive technology, and utilising structured literacy approaches.

Role Modelling Resilience

Role modelling resilience is crucial in support dyslexic pupils and fostering their ability to persevere and overcome challenges. When teachers exhibit resilience themselves and share stories of their own struggles and successes, it can inspire dyslexic pupils to develop a growth mindset and view their difficulties as temporary setbacks rather than permanent limitations (Wolters, 2011). Research has shown that positive teacher modelling of resilience can influence pupils' beliefs about their own abilities and increase their motivation to persist in the face of obstacles (Johnson et al., 2013). By demonstrating resilience and emphasising the importance of effort, perseverance, and learning from mistakes, teachers can instil in dyslexic pupils the belief that they can overcome challenges and achieving success (Dweck, 2006). Through these role modelling efforts, teachers can cultivate a resilient mindset in dyslexic pupils, empowering them to navigate their educational journey with confidence and determination.

Assistive Technology and Accommodations

Teachers can support dyslexic pupils by utilising assistive technology tools and accommodations. These can include text-to-speech software, speech-to-text applications, or access to audiobooks (Hutchison et al., 2012). Such tools and accommodations can facilitate reading, writing, and information processing, empowering dyslexic pupils to overcome challenges and access learning materials effectively.

Universal Design for Learning (UDL)

Implementing Universal Design for Learning principles ensures inclusivity in the classroom. UDL encourages teachers to provide multiple means of representation, expression, and engagement, allowing dyslexic pupils to access information and demonstrate their understanding in various ways (Rose & Meyer, 2002). By providing flexible and supportive learning environments, teachers can cater to diverse learning needs.

Professional Development

Professional development plays a vital role in equipping teachers with the knowledge, skills, and strategies necessary to effectively support dyslexic pupils. Ongoing professional development opportunities allow teachers to stay updated on the latest research and evidence-based practices in dyslexia intervention and instruction (Snowling, 2013). Research suggests that targeted professional development programs focusing on dyslexia can enhance teachers' knowledge, attitudes, and instructional practices (Vaughn et al., 2018). By participating in workshops, conferences, and collaborative learning communities, teachers can acquire a deeper understanding of dyslexia, gain practical strategies for classroom implementation, and engage in reflective practices that enhance their instructional effectiveness (Maddocks & Ballard, 2007). Effective professional development empowers teachers to provide the necessary support, accommodations, and interventions to meet the diverse needs of dyslexic pupils, ultimately enhancing their academic and overall development.

Collaboration with Specialists and Parents

Collaborating with dyslexia specialists and involving parents/guardians as partners is crucial for comprehensive support. By working alongside specialists, teachers can access expert knowledge and guidance in implementing evidence-based interventions (Binks-Cantrell et al., 2011). Engaging parents/guardians fosters open communication, ensuring a shared understanding of dyslexia and facilitating consistency between home and school environments.

By recognising the importance of teacher support and implementing these strategies, educators can empower dyslexic pupils, nurture their strengths, and address their challenges effectively. Through collaborative efforts, teachers can create inclusive classrooms where dyslexic pupils thrive academically, emotionally, and socially.

References

Alexander-Passe, N. (2006). How dyslexic teenagers cope: An investigation of self-esteem, coping and depression. Dyslexia, 12(4), 256-275.

Binks-Cantrell, E. S., et al. (2011). The importance of evidence-based interventions for individuals with dyslexia. International Journal of Speech-Language Pathology, 13(1), 7-10.

British Dyslexia Association (n.d.). What is Dyslexia? Retrieved from https://www.bdadyslexia.org.uk/dyslexic/what-is-dyslexia

Catts, H. W., et al. (2005). Language basis of reading and reading disabilities: Evidence from a longitudinal investigation. Scientific Studies of Reading, 9(3), 167-188.

Cillessen, A. H., & Bellmore, A. D. (2011). Social skills and social acceptance in relation to academic outcomes in middle school children. Journal of Applied School Psychology, 27(2), 184-200.

Critten, S., et al. (2017). Spelling in dyslexic children: Are there particular difficulties with verb inflection? Dyslexia, 23(3), 275-294.

Dowker, A. (2005). Individual differences in arithmetic: Implications for psychology, neuroscience, and education. Psychology Press.

Dweck, C. S. (2006). Mindset: The new psychology of success. Random House.

Fawcett, A. J., & Nicolson, R. I. (1994). Dyslexia and dysgraphia: Neural and genetic factors. In C. Hulme & M. Snowling (Eds.), Dyslexia: Biology, cognition and intervention (pp. 226-238). Lawrence Erlbaum.

Graham, S., & Harris, K. R. (2005). Writing better: Effective strategies for teaching students with learning difficulties. Brookes Publishing.

Geary, D. C. (2004). Mathematics and learning disabilities. Journal of Learning Disabilities, 37(1), 4-15.

Humphrey, N., & Mullins, P. (2002). Personal and situational correlates of peer victimization among children with and without developmental coordination disorder. British Journal of Educational

Psychology, 72(1), 67-83.

Hutchison, L. A., et al. (2012). Assistive technology for students with high-incidence disabilities: Research-based practices. Pearson.

Jiménez, J. E., et al. (2018). Specific learning disabilities and difficulties in literacy and numeracy: A systematic review and meta-analysis. Journal of Research in Special Educational Needs, 18(4), 239-253.

Johnson, S., et al. (2013). Resilient teacher leaders: Teachers who overcome, persevere, and flourish in urban schools. Urban Education, 48(4), 586-615.

MacArthur, C. A., et al. (2016). Teacher-student relationship quality and academic achievement in elementary school: Does dyslexia status matter? Journal of Learning Disabilities, 49(4), 372-385.

McCoach, D. B., et al. (2006). What predicts teachers' attitudes toward the inclusion of students with disabilities in general education classrooms? Teacher Education and Special Education, 29(1), 45-54.

Moll, K., et al. (2016). Math-gender stereotypes and math-related beliefs in childhood and early adolescence. International Journal of Behavioral Development, 40(3), 213-222.

Nation, K., & Snowling, M. J. (2004). Beyond phonological skills: Broader language skills contribute to the development of reading. Journal of Research in Reading, 27(4), 342-356.

National Institute of Child Health and Human Development (n.d.). What is Dyslexia? Retrieved from https://www.nichd.nih.gov/health/topics/dyslexia/conditioninfo

Nippold, M. A., et al. (2005). Language development and reading comprehension: Interconnected pathways to literacy. In H. W. Catts & A. G. Kamhi (Eds.), Language and reading disabilities (2nd ed., pp. 21-48). Allyn & Bacon.

Pemberton, C., & Watkins, A. (2012). Differentiating for specific learning difficulties. SAGE Publications.

Pumfrey, P. D., & Reason, R. (2001). Dyslexia and self-esteem: An exploratory study using the rosenberg self-esteem scale. Dyslexia, 7(2), 87-96.

Rose, D. H., & Meyer, A. (2002). Teaching every student in the digital age: Universal design for learning. ASCD.

Shaywitz, S. E., et al. (1995). Gender differences in the clinical manifestations of dyslexia. Journal of the American Medical

Association, 274(17), 1371-1376.

Shaywitz, S. E., & Shaywitz, B. A. (2008). Paying attention to reading: The neurobiology of reading and dyslexia. Development and Psychopathology, 20(4), 1329-1349.

Sideridis, G. D., et al. (2006). Anxiety symptoms, self-esteem, and social anxiety in children with specific learning disabilities (dyslexia): A cross-cultural study. Journal of Learning Disabilities, 39(3), 248-262.

Snowling, M. J. (2013). Early identification and interventions for dyslexia: A contemporary view. Journal of Research in Special Educational Needs, 13(1), 7-14.

Willcutt, E. G., et al. (2010). The prevalence of DSM-IV attention-deficit/hyperactivity disorder: A meta-analytic review. Neurotherapeutics, 9(3), 490-499.

Wolters, C. A. (2011). Regulation of motivation: Evaluating an underemphasized aspect of self-regulated learning. Educational Psychologist, 46(4), 189-202.

Ziegler, J. C., et al. (2008). Speed of word recognition and vocabulary knowledge in infancy predict cognitive and language outcomes in later childhood. Developmental Science, 11(3), F9-F16.

CHAPTER TWO

Identifying Dyslexia

The identification of dyslexia is a crucial step in providing early intervention and support to individuals. In this chapter, we will explore the process of identifying dyslexia, discussing the various assessment methods, screening tools, and diagnostic criteria used to determine dyslexia in children. We will delve into the importance of early identification, the role of professionals in the assessment process, and the challenges associated with identifying dyslexia accurately. By understanding the complexities of dyslexia identification, educators, clinicians, and other stakeholders can work collaboratively to ensure timely and appropriate interventions that address the unique needs of individuals with dyslexia.

Recognising the Early Signs of Dyslexia

Recognising the early signs of dyslexia is paramount in identifying and supporting individuals with dyslexia in a timely manner. Early identification allows for the implementation of targeted interventions and support that can positively impact long-term outcomes. This section aims to explore the importance of identifying dyslexia early in a child's development and the significance of recognising the early signs as precursors to formal reading instruction.

Pre-Literacy and Pre-School Age Signs

During the pre-literacy and pre-school age period, certain signs may emerge that provide early indications of dyslexia. Recognising these signs is crucial in identifying children at risk and implementing timely interventions. This section will explore the pre-literacy and pre-school age signs associated with dyslexia, emphasising their importance as precursors to formal reading instruction.

- **Language and Speech Delays**

Language and speech delays are often observed in children who later develop dyslexia. Difficulties in vocabulary development, grammar, and pronunciation may become evident during the pre-school years (Snowling et al., 2003). These delays can manifest as challenges in acquiring new words, expressing thoughts coherently, and using appropriate grammatical structures.

- **Phonological Awareness Challenges**

Phonological awareness refers to the ability to recognise and manipulate the sounds of language. Difficulties in this area are considered early markers of dyslexia. Pre-school children at risk of dyslexia may exhibit challenges with rhyming, segmenting, blending, or manipulating individual sounds within words (Muter et al., 2004). These difficulties may become apparent during activities involving nursery rhymes, sound play, or word games.

- **Learning the Alphabet and Letter-Sound Associations**

Dyslexic children may struggle with learning the alphabet and establishing letter-sound associations. They may have difficulty recognising and naming letters, both uppercase and lowercase, as well as linking these letters to their corresponding sounds (Lyytinen et al., 2004). Pre-school children at risk for dyslexia may require additional support and practice to develop these foundational skills.

Early identification of these pre-literacy and pre-school age signs is crucial for implementing targeted interventions and support. It is important for educators, parents, and professionals to be vigilant in observing these signs, as they can provide valuable insights into a child's potential risk for dyslexia. By recognising and addressing these early signs, we can help set dyslexic children on a path to success in reading and writing.

Early School Years Signs

During the early school years, certain signs may become apparent, providing further indications of dyslexia. Recognising these signs is crucial for identifying and supporting children with dyslexia in their academic journey. This section will explore the early school years signs associated with dyslexia, highlighting their significance in informing appropriate interventions.

- ⊚ **Difficulties with Phonics and Decoding Skills**

Dyslexic children often struggle with phonics and decoding skills, which are fundamental for reading. They may have difficulty mapping sounds to letters and blending them to form words (Shaywitz et al., 1999). These challenges can result in slow or inaccurate reading, as well as difficulty reading unfamiliar words (Shaywitz et al., 1992). Despite classroom instruction, dyslexic children may continue to exhibit persistent difficulties in this area.

- ⊚ **Spelling Challenges**

Spelling difficulties are common among dyslexic children. They may struggle with phonetic spelling, inconsistently applying letter-sound relationships, and encountering difficulty in remembering sight words (Bruck, 1990). Dyslexic children may exhibit errors such as omissions, substitutions, and inversions in their written work. These spelling challenges can affect their overall written expression and hinder their ability to convey ideas effectively.

- ⊚ **Challenges in Reading Fluency**

Dyslexia often manifests as difficulties in reading fluency. Dyslexic children may read at a slower pace compared to their peers, have difficulty maintaining a steady reading rhythm, or exhibit a lack of prosody (Shaywitz et al., 1992). They may struggle with word recognition, leading to reading that lacks automaticity and requires significant effort.

- **Written Language Difficulties**

Dyslexic children may encounter challenges in written language expression. These difficulties can include problems with organising thoughts, constructing coherent sentences and paragraphs, and effectively conveying ideas in writing (Berninger et al., 2002). Dyslexic children may exhibit poor handwriting skills, including issues with letter formation, spacing, and overall legibility (Graham et al., 2008).

Identifying these early school years signs is crucial for providing targeted interventions and support to children with dyslexia. By recognising and addressing these challenges, educators, parents, and professionals can help dyslexic children develop the necessary reading and writing skills to succeed academically.

Written Language Challenges

Written language challenges are commonly observed in individuals with dyslexia and can have a significant impact on their ability to express themselves effectively through writing. This section will explore the specific difficulties dyslexic individuals may face in written language and highlight the importance of targeted support and interventions.

- **Organisation and Coherence**

Dyslexic individuals often struggle with organising their thoughts and maintaining coherence in their written work. They may find it challenging to structure sentences, paragraphs, and overall compositions in a logical and cohesive manner (Berninger et al., 2002). Difficulties in organising ideas can result in written pieces that lack clarity and cohesiveness.

- **Spelling Accuracy**

Spelling accuracy is a common area of difficulty for dyslexic individuals. They may struggle with phonetic spelling, finding it challenging to apply consistent letter-sound relationships (Bruck,

1990). Dyslexic individuals may make errors such as omissions, substitutions, or inversions in their written work. These spelling challenges can affect the readability and overall quality of their writing.

● Vocabulary and Word Choice

Dyslexic individuals may encounter challenges in vocabulary acquisition and word choice. They may have difficulty retrieving and using a wide range of words to express their ideas precisely (Berninger et al., 2002). This can result in limited lexical diversity and affect the overall richness of their written expression.

● Sentence Structure and Grammar

Dyslexia can also impact sentence structure and grammatical skills. Dyslexic individuals may struggle with sentence construction, including issues with subject-verb agreement, punctuation, and syntax (Berninger et al., 2002). Difficulties in grammar can affect the clarity and readability of their written work.

Addressing these written language challenges requires targeted interventions and support. Educators and professionals can implement strategies such as:

- ● Providing explicit instruction in organisation and structure, teaching students how to create outlines and use graphic organisers to plan their writing.
- ● Teaching and reinforcing spelling strategies, including mnemonic devices, word families, and spelling rules.
- ● Incorporating vocabulary-building activities, such as word games, contextual reading, and explicit instruction in word meanings and usage.
- ● Offering explicit instruction and practice in sentence structure and grammar, including sentence combining exercises and grammatical rules.

By providing targeted support in these areas, dyslexic individuals can develop their written language skills, enhance their written expression, and effectively convey their ideas.

Cognitive and Memory Factors

Cognitive and Memory Factors plays a significant role in dyslexia and can contribute to the challenges individuals with dyslexia face in reading, writing, and overall academic performance. This section will explore the cognitive and memory factors associated with dyslexia, shedding light on their impact and implications for interventions and support.

◉ **Working Memory Difficulties**

Dyslexic individuals often experience difficulties with working memory, which refers to the ability to temporarily hold and manipulate information in the mind. Working memory plays a crucial role in tasks such as following multi-step instructions, remembering, and applying phonics rules, and comprehending complex sentences (Swanson & Siegel, 2001). Dyslexic individuals may struggle with tasks that require holding information in memory while simultaneously performing other cognitive processes, which can affect their reading comprehension and overall learning.

◉ **Processing Speed**

Processing speed refers to the speed at which an individual can process and respond to information. Dyslexic individuals may exhibit slower processing speed compared to their peers (Wolf & Bowers, 1999). This slower processing speed can impact various academic tasks, including reading, writing, and problem-solving. It may contribute to difficulties in completing assignments within time constraints, affecting overall productivity and performance.

◉ **Attention and Executive Functions**

Dyslexic individuals may experience challenges related to attention and executive functions. Executive functions encompass cognitive processes such as attentional control, cognitive flexibility, and inhibitory control. Difficulties in these areas can impact self-regulation, planning, organising, and sustaining attention during academic tasks (Willcutt et al., 2010). These challenges can further exacerbate reading and writing difficulties, as well as overall task completion.

Addressing cognitive and memory factors requires targeted

interventions and support that accommodate the specific needs of dyslexic individuals. Some strategies that can be beneficial include:

- Providing explicit instruction and practice in developing working memory skills, such as chunking information, using mnemonic techniques, and implementing strategies for organising and remembering information.
- Allowing additional processing time during academic tasks and assessments to accommodate slower processing speed.
- Incorporating strategies to enhance attention and executive functions, such as breaking tasks into smaller, manageable steps, providing visual cues or prompts, and teaching self-regulation techniques.

By recognising and addressing these cognitive and memory factors, educators and professionals can help dyslexic individuals overcome barriers, optimise their learning potential, and promote academic success.

Social and Emotional Indicators

Social and emotional well-being are significant aspects of a dyslexic individual's overall development. Dyslexia can have implications for social interactions, self-perception, and emotional experiences. This section will explore the social and emotional indicators associated with dyslexia, highlighting their impact and the importance of addressing these factors in supporting dyslexic individuals.

- **Frustration and Self-Esteem**

Dyslexic individuals often experience frustration due to the challenges they encounter in reading, writing, and other academic tasks. Persistent difficulties can lead to feelings of inadequacy and lower self-esteem (Riddick, 2006). These negative emotions can further impact their motivation, engagement, and overall well-being.

- **Peer Interactions and Social Acceptance**

Dyslexic individuals may encounter difficulties in peer interactions and social acceptance. They may experience challenges in keeping up with their peers academically, leading to potential feelings of being difference or excluded (Alexander-Passe, 2006). These experiences can affect their sense of belonging, self-confidence, and overall social integration.

◎ Anxiety and Avoidance

Anxiety related to dyslexia is not uncommon, as dyslexic individuals may worry about reading aloud, spelling errors, or being stigmatised due to their difficulties (Hutchinson & Carroll, 2010). This anxiety can manifest as avoidance behaviours, where individual may shy away from participating in activities that highlight their challenges, such as reading in front of others or engaging in written assignments.

Addressing social and emotional indicators is vital to support the well-being and academic success of dyslexic individuals. Strategies that can be beneficial in this regard include:

- ◎ Creating a supportive and inclusive classroom environment that fosters empathy, understanding, and acceptance of differences.
- ◎ Incorporating strengths-based approaches, recognising and building upon dyslexic individuals' talents and abilities.
- ◎ Implementing interventions to enhance self-esteem and self-confidence, such as providing opportunities for success, celebrating achievements, and encouraging a growth mindset.
- ◎ Promoting social skills development through targeted instruction, peer collaboration, and fostering positive peer relationships.
- ◎ Offering access to appropriate support services, such as counselling or social-emotional learning programs, to address anxiety and emotional well-being.

By addressing social and emotional indicators, educators, parents, and professionals can help dyslexic individuals navigate their educational journey with increased confidence, resilience, and positive social interactions.

Collaborative Assessment and Monitoring

Collaborative assessment and monitoring are essential components in identifying and supporting individuals with dyslexia. This section explores the significance of a collaborative approach among educators, professionals, and parents in conducting comprehensive assessments and ongoing monitoring to ensure appropriate interventions and support.

⊚ Collaborative Assessment

Collaborative assessment involves a multi-faceted approach that considers various aspects of dyslexia, including cognitive, linguistic, and educational factors. This collaborative process typically includes input from educators, specialised professionals (e.g. speech-language pathologists, psychologists), and parent/guardians. By working together, these stakeholders can contribute their unique perspectives, knowledge, and expertise to develop a holistic understanding of the individual's strengths and challenges.

⊚ Shared Information and Observations

Collaboration allows for the sharing of information and observations from multiple sources. Educators can provide insights into the student's academic performance, behaviour, and progress within the classroom setting. Parents/guardians can contribute valuable information regarding the child's developmental history, family context, and their observations of the child's struggles or strengths at home. Specialists can conduct specific assessments to evaluate cognitive and linguistic abilities, identify areas of difficulty, and provide recommendations for appropriate interventions.

⊚ Ongoing Monitoring

Collaborative monitoring involves regular communication and follow-up among stakeholders to track the progress of dyslexic individuals. This monitoring can include assessing academic performance, evaluating the effectiveness of interventions, and identifying any emerging needs. Collaboration allows for the identification of potential challenges or barriers and the timely adjustment of support strategies to meet the evolving needs of the individual.

- **Consistency Between Home and School**

Collaboration between parents/guardians and educators ensures consistency between the home and school environments. By sharing information, strategies, and resources, parents/guardians and educators can align their approaches, reinforcing the support provided to the dyslexic individual. This consistency enhances the effectiveness of interventions and reinforces the individual's understanding that their support network is working together towards their success.

- **Access to Specialised Support**

Collaboration facilitates access to specialised support services. By working collaboratively, educators and parents/guardians can seek guidance from dyslexia specialists, such as educational psychologists or dyslexia tutors. These professionals can provide further assessments, offer targeted intervention strategies, and share evidence-based practices to enhance support for dyslexic individuals.

Collaborative assessment and monitoring foster a comprehensive understanding of the dyslexic individual's needs, ensuring appropriate interventions and support. By working together, educators, professionals, and parents/guardians can optimise the individual's learning experience, promote their progress, and empower them to achieve their full potential.

By recognising the early signs of dyslexia, educators and parents can take proactive steps to provide appropriate interventions and support, leading to improved outcomes for individuals with dyslexia.

Screening and Assessment

Screening and assessments are vital components in identifying and supporting individuals with dyslexia. This section provides an introduction to the importance of screening and assessments in the context of dyslexia, emphasising their role in early identification, intervention planning, and educational decision-making. We will explore the purpose of screening tools and assessments, the benefits they offer, and the collaborative process involving educators, professionals, and parents in conducting comprehensive evaluations. By understanding the significance of screening and assessments, stake holders can work together to ensure accurate identification, appropriate interventions, and tailored support for individuals with dyslexia.

Screening for Dyslexia

Screening for dyslexia is a crucial step in identifying individuals who may be at risk of dyslexia and require further assessment and support. This section explores the purpose of screening, commonly used screening tools and methods, and the collaborative approach involved in the screening process.

⊛ Purpose of Screening

Screening serves as an initial evaluation to identify individuals who may exhibit signs and risk factors associated with dyslexia. The primary purpose of screening is to determine whether further assessment is needed to confirm the presence of dyslexia and to guide appropriate interventions. Early identification through screening allows for timely support and intervention, which can significantly impact an individual's academic progress (Shaywitz, 1998).

⊛ Screening Tools and Methods

Various screening tools and methods are available to access key skills and indicators associated with dyslexia. These tools aim to identify potential difficulties in areas such as phonological awareness, rapid automatised naming, letter-sound knowledge, and other cognitive and language abilities (Snowling et al., 2003). Commonly used screening methods include standardised tests, checklists, and observations. Standardised tests provide a structured and objective assessment, while checklists and observations offer a more qualitative evaluation of behaviours and characteristics associated with dyslexia.

⊛ Collaborative Approach in Screening

Collaboration is essential in the screening process for dyslexia. Educators, professionals, and parents work together to administer screening tools, interpret results, and determine the next steps.

Educators play a critical role in providing valuable insights into the student's academic performance, classroom behaviour, and areas of difficulty. Professionals, such as psychologists, speech-language pathologists, or dyslexia specialists, contribute their expertise in administering and interpreting screening tool. Parents' input is crucial, as they can provide information about the child's developmental history, behaviours outside of the school setting, and observations of their strengths and struggles. By working collaboratively, stakeholders can gather a comprehensive understanding of the individual's profile and make informed decisions regarding further assessment intervention.

Screening for dyslexia plays a vital role in identifying individuals who may require additional evaluation and support. By implementing screening procedures, educators, professionals, and parents can identify potential signs of dyslexia early on, allowing for timely intervention and tailored support. The collaborative approach ensures a comprehensive evaluation and shared understanding of the individual's needs, leading to effective intervention strategies and improved outcomes.

Comprehensive Assessments

Comprehensive assessments play a crucial role in evaluating dyslexia by providing a detailed understanding of an individual's strengths, weaknesses, and specific areas of difficulty. This section explores the purpose of comprehensive assessments, the assessment methods used, and the collaborative approach involved in conducting these evaluations.

⊚ **Purpose of Comprehensive Assessments**

Comprehensive assessments are designed to gather extensive information about an individual's cognitive, linguistic, and educational abilities related to dyslexia. The purpose of these assessments is to obtain a comprehensive understanding of the individual's profile, identify the presence and severity of dyslexic characteristics, and guide intervention planning (Mather & Wendling, 2012). By examining various domains, comprehensive assessments enable professionals to identify specific areas of difficulty and tailor interventions to meet the individual's needs.

◉ Assessment Methods

Comprehensive assessments employ a range of methods to evaluate different aspects of dyslexia. These methods include cognitive assessments, reading and writing assessments, language evaluations, and other related measures. Cognitive assessments assess cognitive abilities such as intelligence, processing speed, memory, and executive functions. Reading and writing assessments examine specific reading and writing skills, decoding abilities, fluency, reading comprehension, and written expression. Language evaluations assess language skills, including phonological awareness, vocabulary, grammar, and comprehension (Fletcher et al., 2007). These assessment methods provide a comprehensive overview of the individual's strengths and weaknesses, guiding intervention planning and support.

◉ Collaborative Approach in Comprehensive Assessments

Comprehensive assessments for dyslexia involve a collaborative approach among educators, professionals, and parents. Educators contribute their knowledge and observations of the individual's academic performance, classroom behaviour, and specific challenges. Professionals, such as educational psychologists, speech-language pathologists, and dyslexia specialists, administer and interpret assessments, providing their expertise in identifying dyslexic characteristics and making appropriate recommendations. Parents' input is invaluable, as they provide information about the child's developmental history, behaviours outside of the school setting, and personal observations. By working collaboratively, these stakeholders gain a holistic understanding of the individual ensuring a comprehensive evaluation and facilitating targeted interventions.

Comprehensive assessments provide a comprehensive understanding of an individual's strengths, weaknesses, and specific areas of difficulty related to dyslexia. These assessments guide intervention planning, tailored support, and educational decision-making. The collaborative approach ensures a comprehensive evaluation that integrates insights from educators, professionals, and parents, resulting in informed decisions and effective interventions for individuals with dyslexia.

Diagnosis and Educational Decision-Making

The process of diagnosing dyslexia and making educational decision is a crucial step in providing appropriate interventions and support for individuals with dyslexia. This section explores the diagnostic criteria commonly used in the United Kingdom, the educational implications of a dyslexia diagnosis, and the importance of collaboration in decision-making.

⊚ **Diagnostic Criteria for Dyslexia**

In the UK, the British Dyslexia Association (BDA) provides guidance on diagnosing dyslexia. The BDA considers dyslexia as a specific learning difficulty that primarily affects reading and spelling skills. The diagnostic criteria include persistent difficulties in phonological processing, verbal memory, processing speed, and literacy skills significantly below age-appropriate expectations. The diagnosis also takes into account the impact of these difficulties on academic achievement and daily functioning. Diagnostic assessments can only be carried out by qualified assessors.

⊚ **Educational Implications**

A formal diagnosis of dyslexia has significant implications for educational planning and support. It helps to identify the specific learning needs and challenges of the individual, enabling the development of tailored interventions, accommodations, and strategies. Educational implications may include access to specialised dyslexia support, reasonable adjustments within the educational setting, and additional support services such as dyslexia tutoring or assistive technology. A dyslexia diagnosis ensures eligibility for reasonable adjustments and support in accordance with the Equality Act 2010 and the Special Educational Needs and Disability (SEND) Code of Practice.

⊚ **Collaborative Decision-Making**

Collaboration among educators, professionals, and parents is crucial in making informed decisions regarding educational interventions for individuals with dyslexia. Educators provide valuable insights into the pupil's academic performance, progress, and response to interventions within the educational context. Professionals, such as educational psychologists, dyslexia specialists, or speech and language therapists, contribute their expertise in interpreting assessment results and recommending appropriate interventions. Parents' input is essential, as they offer insights into the child's strengths, challenges, and personal experiences. By working collaboratively, stakeholders can ensure that decisions are well-informed, considering the specific needs and support available.

The diagnosis of dyslexia informs educational decision-making by guiding the development of personalised intervention plans and support strategies. It ensures that individuals with dyslexia receive the necessary accommodations, targeted instruction, and resources to support their learning and academic success. Collaboration among educators, professionals, and parents is fundamental in navigating the education system, promoting the well-being and optimising the potential of individuals with dyslexia.

Benefits and Limitations of Screening and Assessments

Screening and assessments play a crucial role in identifying and understanding dyslexia, but it is important to recognise both their benefits and limitations. This section explores the advantages and potential drawbacks of screening and assessments.

- ◉ **Benefits of Screening and Assessments**
    - o Early identification – *Screening enables early identification of individuals who may be at risk of dyslexia, allowing for timely intervention and support. Early identification is crucial for implementing targeted interventions that can positively impact an individual's academic progress (Shaywitz, 1998).*
    - o Tailored Interventions – *Assessments provide a comprehensive understanding of an individual's strengths, weaknesses, and specific areas of difficulty. This information*

guides the development of tailored interventions and support strategies to address the unique needs of individuals with dyslexia.

o Evidence-Based Decision Making – *Screening and assessments provide objective data that inform educational decision-making. They help identify the presence and severity of dyslexic characteristics, assisting educators, professionals, and parents in making informed choices regarding appropriate interventions and accommodations.*

◉ **Limitations of Screening and Assessments**

o False Positives and Negatives – *Screening may result in false positives (identifying individuals as at risk when they do not have dyslexia) or false negatives (failing to identify individuals with dyslexia). It is crucial to consider multiple sources of information and use screening results as a starting point for further assessments and evaluations.*

o Individual Variability – *Dyslexia is a complex condition with significant individual variability. Assessments may not capture the full extent of an individual's strengths, weaknesses, or specific challenges. It is essential to consider assessment results in conjunction with other observations, such as classroom performance and personal experiences.*

o Dynamic Nature of Dyslexia – *Dyslexia can evolve over time, and individuals may exhibit different strengths and weaknesses as they develop. Assessments provide a snapshot of an individual's abilities at a specific point in time, and ongoing monitoring is necessary to track progress, identify emerging needs, and adjust interventions accordingly.*

◉ **Importance of Collaboration and Context**

Collaboration among educators, professionals, and parents is vital in interpreting screening and assessment results. Different stakeholders bring valuable insights and expertise, contributing to a comprehensive understanding of the individual's profile. Additionally, the interpretation of screening and assessment results should be contextualised within the specific educational, cultural, and linguistic environment of the individual.

By acknowledging the benefits and limitations of screening and assessments, stakeholders can make informed decisions and develop holistic support plans for individuals with dyslexia. Collaboration and ongoing monitoring enhance the effectiveness of interventions, ensuring that individuals receive the appropriate support to thrive academically and personally.

By understanding the purpose, methods, and collaborative nature of screening and assessments for dyslexia, stakeholders can work together to ensure accurate identification, appropriate interventions, and tailored support for individuals with dyslexia.

Creating a Supportive Classroom Environment

Creating a supportive classroom environment is paramount to ensuring the success and well-being of students with dyslexia. By establishing an inclusive and positive atmosphere, educators can factor a sense of belonging, enhancing learning experiences, and empower students to reach their full potential. This section explores strategies and practises that contribute to building a supportive classroom environment for students with dyslexia. From building rapport and empathy, accommodations, and assistive technologies, as well as promoting self-advocacy and collaboration with parents and professionals, educators can create an environment where students with dyslexia thrive academically, develop confidence, and embrace their unique strengths. By prioritising a supportive classroom environment, educators play a vital role in nurturing the growth and success of students with dyslexia.

Building Rapport and Empathy

Building rapport and empathy is a foundational aspect of creating a supportive classroom environment for pupils with dyslexia. By cultivating a positive relationship and fostering empathy, educators can establish a safe and inclusive space where students feel understood, valued, and supported. This section explores strategies and practices that promote rapport and empathy in the classroom, drawing upon research and educational expertise.

- **Establishing a Positive Teacher-Student Relationship**
  - oActive Listening – *actively listening to students fosters a sense of trust and understanding (Marzano, 2003). Research suggests that attentive listening improves teacher-student relationships and enhances students' academic engagement (Roorda et al., 2011).*
  - oRespect and Validation – *demonstrating respect for students' ideas, thoughts, and emotions is crucial for building rapport (Jones et al., 2019). Validating students' experiences fosters a sense of belonging and promotes positive relationships (Cornelius-White, 2007).*
  - oApproachability and Availability – *being approachable and available to students establishes open lines of communication and encourages students to seek support when needed (Aldridge & Fraser, 2015).*

- **Fostering a Safe and Non-Judgemental Space**
  - oEstablishing classroom norms – *collaboratively developing classroom norms that promote respect, kindness, and inclusivity creates a safe environment (Freiberg, 2002). Clear expectations contribute to a positive classroom climate.*
  - oAnti-bully Practices – *implementing anti-bullying strategies and promoting empathy helps create a safe and non-judgemental space (Orpinas & Horne, 2006). Addressing bullying behaviours supports the emotional well-being of all students.*
  - oCultivating a Growth Mindset – *fostering a growth mindset culture encourages resilience, effort, and a belief in the ability to improve (Dweck, 2006). A growth mindset fosters a positive learning environment where mistakes are seen as opportunities for growth.*

- **Promoting Peer Relationships and Collaboration**
  - oGroup Activities and Projects – *collaborative activities and*

projects provide opportunities for students to work together, fostering positive peer relationships (Johnson & Johnson, 2014). Cooperative learning enhances social interaction and promotes empathy.

o Cooperative Learning Strategies – *implementing cooperative learning strategies, such as peer tutoring or group discussions, allows students to support and learn from one another (Slavin, 1996). Cooperative learning improves academic achievement and enhances social skills.*

o Inclusive Classroom Culture – *fostering an inclusive classroom culture that values diversity and encourages understanding of different perspectives promotes empathy and positive social interactions (Topping & Ehly, 1998).*

◉ **Cultivating Empathy and Understanding**

o Empathy Exercises – *engaging students in empathy-building exercises, such as literature discussions or community service projects, helps develop empathy towards others (Battistich et al., 2004). Promoting empathy contributes to a supportive classroom environment.*

o Awareness of Strengths – *helping students recognise and appreciate their own strengths while fostering understanding of diverse strengths among their peers promotes positive relationships (Noddings, 2005). Appreciating diverse strengths creates a culture of acceptance and support.*

By prioritising the building of rapport and empathy, educators create an environment where students with dyslexia feel supported, valued, and empowered. This foundation sets the stage for meaningful learning experiences and encourages students to embrace their challenges, collaborate with peers, and research their full potential.

Accommodations and Assistive Technologies

Accommodations and assistive technologies are essential components of creating an inclusive and supportive classroom environment for students with dyslexia. By implementing appropriate accommodations and utilising assistive technologies, educators can address specific learning needs, facilitate access to the curriculum, and empower students with dyslexia to demonstrate their knowledge and abilities. This section explores a range of accommodations and assistive technologies that can enhance the learning experience for students with dyslexia.

- **Accommodations for Reading and Writing**
    - Extended Time – *providing extended time for reading and writing tasks allows students with dyslexia to process information and express their thoughts more effectively (National Centre for Learning Disabilities, 2021).*
    - Modified Assignments – *modifying assignments to accommodate the specific needs of learners with dyslexia, such as reducing the length or complexity of reading passages or providing alternative writing formats, helps ensure their active participation and success (Understood, 2021).*
    - Preferential Seating – *allowing students with dyslexia to sit in a location that minimises distractions and supports their visual access to instruction can enhance their focus and engagement (American Speech-Language-Hearing Association, 2018).*

- **Assistive Technologies for Reading and Writing**
    - Test-to-Speech Software – *text-to-speech software converts written text into spoken words, enabling students with dyslexia to access and comprehend written material more effectively (Assistive Technology Industry Association, n.d.)*
    - Speech Recognition Software – *speech recognition software allows students to dictate their thoughts and ideas, which is particularly beneficial for those with dyslexia who struggle with writing or spelling (CAST, n.d.).*
    - Word Prediction Tools – *word prediction tools suggest words or phrases as students type, supporting their writing process and reducing spelling errors (Learning Disabilities Association of America, n.d.).*
    - Electronic Organisers and Note-Taking Apps – *electronic*

organisers and note-taking apps help students with dyslexia manage their assignments, schedules, and class notes more efficiently (National Center on Accessible Educational Materials, n.d.).

- ◉ **Environmental Accommodations**
  - o Visual Aids and Graphic Organisers – *utilising visual aids, such as charts, diagrams, and graphic organisers, helps students with dyslexia organise information and enhance their understanding of complex concepts (Understood, 2021).*
  - o Multisensory Instruction – *incorporating multisensory instruction techniques, such as using manipulatives, gestures, or sensory materials, engages multiple senses to reinforce learning and enhance memory retrieval (International Dyslexia Association, 2021).*
  - o Noise Reduction Strategies – *implementing noise reduction strategies, such as using headphones or providing a quiet workspace, minimises auditory distractions for students with dyslexia, improving their focus and concentration (National Center for Learning Disabilities, 2021).*

- ◉ **Accessibility and Universal Design**
  - o Accessible Materials – *providing accessible materials, such as digital texts with adjustable font sizes and dyslexia-friendly formatting, ensure equitable access to information for students with dyslexia (Center on Technology and Disability, 2019).*
  - o Universal Design for Learning (UDL) – *applying UDL principles, which emphasise multiple means of representation, engagement, and expression, benefits all learners, including those with dyslexia, by providing flexible learning options that suit individual needs (CAST, 2018).*

By implementing accommodations and utilising assistive technologies, educators can level the playing field for students with dyslexia, promoting their active participation and success in the classroom. These strategies not only support their specific learning needs but also foster independence, confidence, and a positive attitude towards learning.

Encouraging Self-Advocacy and Confidence

Encouraging self-advocacy and fostering confidence are crucial aspects of supporting students with dyslexia in the classroom. By empowering students to understand their strengths, advocate for their needs, and develop a positive self-image, educators can promote their overall well-being and academic success. This section explores strategies and practices that facilitate self-advocacy and confidence building for students with dyslexia.

- **Building Self-Awareness**
  - Strengths-Based Approach – *help students recognise and celebrate their unique strengths and talents. By focusing on their abilities and positive attributes, students develop a more positive self-image and become more motivated and overcome challenges (Smith, 2018).*
  - Reflective Activities – *engage students in reflective activities, such as journaling or self-assessments, to increase self-awareness about their learning preferences, challenges, and strategies that work best for them (Swanson, 2021).*
  - Personalised Goal Setting – *collaborate with students to set individualised goals that target their specific needs and aspirations. This process helps students take ownership of their learning and foster a sense of control over their academic journey (Kauffman et al., 2017).*

- **Developing Self-Advocacy Skills**
  - Knowledge and Dyslexia – *educate students about dyslexia, helping them understand their learning differences and how it affects their academic experience. This knowledge empowers students to communicate their needs effectively and seek appropriate support (Shaywitz, 2003).*
  - Self-Advocacy Instruction – *teach students specific self-advocacy skills, such as asking for accommodations,*

seeking clarification, or expressing their learning preferences. Provide opportunities for role-playing and practicing assertive communication (Moats, 2010).

o Collaborative Problem-Solving – *encourage students to actively participate in problem-solving discussions and decision-making processes regarding their learning needs. This collaborative approach reinforces their sense of agency and promotes self-advocacy (Hunt & Szymanski, 2020).*

⊚ **Nurturing Self-Confidence**

o Strength-Based Feedback – *provide specific and constructive feedback that focuses on students' strengths, efforts, and progress. Celebrate their achievements, both big and small, to boost their confidence and motivation (Dweck, 2006).*

o Growth Mindset Culture – *foster a growth mindset culture that emphasises the belief in the capacity to learn and improve. Encourage students to view mistakes as opportunities for growth and to embrace challenges as steppingstones to success (Blackwell et al., 2007).*

o Success Experiences – *create opportunities for students to experience success in areas where they excel. This could involve assigning tasks that align with their strengths or providing them with leadership roles in group projects (Wang et al., 2020).*

⊚ **Creating Supportive Learning Environment**

o Safe and Non-Judgemental Space – *foster a classroom environment where students feel safe to take risks, make mistakes, and ask for help without fear of judgement. Promote a culture of respect, acceptance, and support among peers (Bennett et al., 2019).*

o Collaborative Partnerships – *engage in open communication and collaboration with parents, providing them with resources and strategies to support their child's self-advocacy and confidence-building efforts. Collaborating with parents fosters a unified support system for students (Bender & Schmitt, 2019).*

By encouraging self-advocacy and fostering confidence, educators play a vital role in empowering students with dyslexia to take control of their learning journey. Through a strengths-based approach, explicit instruction in self-advocacy skills, nurturing self-confidence, and creating a supportive environment, students develop the resilience and belief in their abilities to overcome challenges and achieve their full potential.

Collaborating with Parents and Professionals

Collaborating with parents can professionals is a crucial component of supporting students with dyslexia. By establishing strong partnerships and open lines of communication, educators can gain valuable insights, share information, and work together to create a comprehensive support system for students. This section explores strategies and practices for effective collaboration with parents and professionals to enhance the educational experiences and outcomes for students with dyslexia.

- **Establishing Collaborative Relationships with Parents**
  - Open and Frequent Communication – *maintain regular communication with parents to exchange information about students' progress, challenges, and strategies for support. Utilise various channels, such as emails, phone calls, newsletters, and parent-teacher conferences, to keep parents informed and involved (Epstein, 2011).*
  - Actively Listen and Validate – *practice active listening when engaging with parents, allowing them to share their concerns, perspectives, and insights about their child's strengths and challenges. Show empathy, respect, and validation for their experiences and input (Rumberger et al., 2003).*
  - Involve Parents in Decision-Making – *collaborate with parents in the decision-making process regarding interventions, accommodations, and individualised education plans (IEPs). Seek their input, consider their expertise, and involve them as partners in setting goals and planning for their child's educational journey (Turnbull et al., 2016).*

◉ **Sharing Information and Resources**

　o Parent Education and Workshops – *provide workshops, training sessions, or informational resources to help parents better understand dyslexia, its impact on learning, and effective strategies for support. Empower parents with knowledge and tools to advocate for their child's needs (Hudson et al., 2015).*

　o Resource Sharing – *share educational resources, articles, books, and websites with parents to broaden their understanding of dyslexia and provide access to evidence-based practices and interventions (National Center for Learning Disabilities, 2021).*

　o Home-School Collaboration – *encourage parents to share insights about their child's learning experiences at home and provide suggestions for reinforcement and support. Collaboratively establish consistent strategies and routines between home and school to promote continuity in learning (Desimone & Davis-Kean, 2005).*

◉ **Collaborating with Professionals**

　o Interdisciplinary Collaboration – *foster collaboration with professionals such as special education teachers, speech and language therapists, and educational psychologists. Share relevant information, assessments, and observations to create a holistic understanding of student's needs and develop targeted interventions (Friend & Cook, 2020).*

　o Regular Team Meetings – *schedule regular team meetings to discuss student progress, review interventions, and coordinate strategies across different educational settings. This collaborative approach ensures a coordinated and cohesive support system for the student (Odom et al., 2020).*

　o Professional Development and Training – *engage in professional development opportunities that enhance collaboration skills, cultural competence, and understanding of diverse learning needs. Build a shared knowledge base among professionals to facilitate effective collaboration (National Joint Committee on Learning Disabilities, 2015).*

◉ **Respecting Cultural and Linguistic Diversity**

 oCultural Responsiveness – *recognise and respect the cultural background and values of families. Develop cultural competence to understand how cultural factors may influence students' experiences and approaches to learning (Harry et al., 2005).*

 oLanguage Support – *provide language support for parents who may have limited English proficiency. Utilise interpreters, translated materials, or bilingual professionals to ensure effective communication and meaningful participation (Reese et al., 2010).*

By fostering collaboration with parents and professionals, educators can create a comprehensive and cohesive support system for students with dyslexia. Collaborative partnerships empower parents as active advocates and contributors to their child's education, while interdisciplinary collaboration ensures a unified approach to meeting students' diverse needs.

By creating a supportive classroom environment, educators can empower students with dyslexia to thrive academically, develop their strengths, and build confidence. Implementing strategies such as building rapport, differentiated instruction, accommodations, assistive technologies, fostering self-advocacy, and collaboration with parents and professionals contribute to a positive and inclusive learning environment for all students.

References

Aldridge, J. M., & Fraser, B. J. (2015). Classroom environment and student outcomes: What we know and what we need to know. In B. J. Fraser, K. G. Tobin, & C. J. McRobbie (Eds.), Second International Handbook of Science Education (pp. 1191-1212). Springer.

American Speech-Language-Hearing Association. (2018). Preferred practice patterns for the profession of speech-language pathology. Retrieved from https://www.asha.org/Practice/recommended-practice-patterns/

Alexander-Passe, N. (2006). How dyslexic teenagers cope: An investigation of self-esteem, coping and depression. Dyslexia, 12(4), 256-275.

Assistive Technology Industry Association. (n.d.). Text-to-speech (TTS). Retrieved from https://www.atia.org/assistive-technology/assistive-technology-ideas/text-to-speech-tts/

Battistich, V., et al. (2004). Schools as communities, poverty levels of student populations, and students' attitudes, motives, and performance: A multilevel analysis. American Educational Research Journal, 41(4), 797-823.

Bennett, A., et al. (2019). Creating safe spaces for students to learn. Teaching Exceptional Children, 51(5), 314-321.

Bender, W. N., & Schmitt, L. (2019). Parental advocacy: The cornerstone of special education. Council for Exceptional Children.

Berninger, V. W., et al. (2002). Treatment of handwriting problems in beginning writers: Transfer from handwriting to composition. Journal of Educational Psychology, 94(4), 686-701.

Blackwell, L. S., et al. (2007). Implicit theories of intelligence predict achievement across an adolescent transition: A longitudinal study and an intervention. Child Development, 78(1), 246-263.

British Dyslexia Association. (n.d.). Dyslexia assessment. https://www.bdadyslexia.org.uk/dyslexic/dyslexia-assessment

Bruck, M. (1990). Word-recognition skills of adults with childhood diagnoses of dyslexia. Developmental Psychology, 26(3), 439-454.

CAST. (n.d.). Speech recognition. Retrieved from http://www.cast.org/our-work/research-development/joy-of-reading/technology-to-support-reading-and-writing/speech-recognition.html

Center on Technology and Disability. (2019). Accessible educational materials. Retrieved from https://www.ctdinstitute.org/library/2020-08-25/accessible-educational-materials-aems

Cornelius-White, J. (2007). Learner-centered teacher-student relationships are effective: A meta-analysis. Review of Educational Research, 77(1), 113-143.

Department for Education. (2015). SEND code of practice: 0 to 25 years. https://assets.publishing.service.gov.uk/government/uploads/system/u

ploads/attachment_data/file/398815/SEND_Code_of_Practice_January_2015.pdf

Desimone, L. M., & Davis-Kean, P. E. (2005). Influences on parents' and schools' support of children's math interests and self-beliefs. Journal of Educational Research, 98(4), 208-222.

Dweck, C. S. (2006). Mindset: The new psychology of success. Ballantine Books.

Epstein, J. L. (2011). School, family, and community partnerships: Preparing educators and improving schools. Westview Press.

Equality Act. (2010). http://www.legislation.gov.uk/ukpga/2010/15/contents

Fletcher, J. M., et al. (2007). Classification of learning disabilities: An evidence-based evaluation. In H. L. Swanson, K. R. Harris, & S. Graham (Eds.), Handbook of Learning Disabilities (pp. 77-98). Guilford Press.

Freiberg, H. J. (2002). Creating a caring community in the classroom. In C. M. Evertson & C. S. Weinstein (Eds.), Handbook of Classroom Management: Research, Practice, and Contemporary Issues (pp. 543-570). Routledge.

Friend, M., & Cook, L. (2020). Interactions: Collaboration skills for school professionals. Pearson.

Graham, S., et al. (2008). Teaching handwriting: A stroke-based approach for children with dyslexia. Exceptionality, 16(4), 243-265.

Harry, B., et al. (2005). Collaborative Home-School Interventions: Evidence-Based Solutions for Emotional, Behavioral, and Academic Problems. Guilford Press.

Hudson, R. F., et al. (2015). Using parent-friendly knowledge to increase parent involvement in early literacy: Two experimental studies. School Psychology Review, 44(3), 302-315.

Hunt, P., & Szymanski, C. (2020). Self-advocacy instruction: A critical component of education for students with disabilities. TEACHING Exceptional Children, 52(1), 41-50.

Hutchinson, N. L., & Carroll, J. M. (2010). Dyslexia-friendly further and higher education. Sage Publications.

International Dyslexia Association. (2021). Dyslexia basics. Retrieved from https://dyslexiaida.org/dyslexia-basics/

Johnson, D. W., & Johnson, R. T. (2014). Cooperative learning in 21st century. Anales de Psicología, 30(3), 841-851.

Jones, S. M., et al. (2019). The role of teacher emotional support in sustaining high-need schools. Policy Insights from the Behavioral and Brain Sciences, 6(1), 107-114.

Kauffman, J. M., et al. (2017). Goals and goal setting in the individualized education program. In J. W. Lloyd, J. K. Kauffman, & S. L. Martin (Eds.), Handbook of Instructional Practices for Literacy Teacher-educators: Examples and Reflections From the Teaching Lives of Literacy Scholars (pp. 186-200). Routledge.

Learning Disabilities Association of America. (n.d.). Technology supports and accommodations for writing. Retrieved from https://ldaamerica.org/types-of-technology-supports-and-accommodations-for-writing/

Lyytinen, H., et al. (2004). Early identification and prevention of dyslexia: Results from a prospective follow-up study of children at familial risk for dyslexia. Journal of Learning Disabilities, 37(4), 357-377.

Marzano, R. J. (2003). What works in schools: Translating research into action. ASCD.

Mather, N., & Wendling, B. J. (2012). Essentials of dyslexia assessment and intervention. John Wiley & Sons.

Moats, L. C. (2010). Dyslexia: Strategies for teachers and parents. Perspectives on Language and Literacy, 36(2), 18-22.

Muter, V., et al. (2004). Phonological sensitivity deficits in developmental dyslexia and the phonological representations hypothesis. Journal of Experimental Child Psychology, 87(4), 299-319.

National Center for Learning Disabilities. (2021). Assistive technology for kids with learning disabilities: An overview. Retrieved from https://www.understood.org/en/school-learning/assistive-technology/assistive-technologies-basics/assistive-technology-for-kids-with-learning-disabilities-an-overview

National Center for Learning Disabilities. (2021). Parent-teacher partnerships: A toolkit for dyslexia. Retrieved from https://www.ncld.org/wp-content/uploads/2021/05/NCLD-PT-Partnerships-Toolkit.pdf

National Center on Accessible Educational Materials. (n.d.). Organizers, graphic organizers, mind mapping. Retrieved from https://aem.cast.org/creating/course/view.php?id=80

National Joint Committee on Learning Disabilities. (2015). National Joint Committee on Learning Disabilities position statement: Principles for identification and instruction of students with specific learning disabilities. Retrieved from https://www.asha.org/siteassets/advocacy/position-statements/principl es-for-identification-and-instruction-of-students-with-specific-learning -disabilities.pdf

Noddings, N. (2005). The challenge to care in schools: An alternative approach to education (2nd ed.). Teachers College Press.

Odom, S. L., et al. (2020). Collaborating for effective inclusive education: International perspectives. Routledge.

Orpinas, P., & Horne, A. M. (2006). Bullying prevention: Creating a positive school climate and developing social competence. American Psychological Association.

Reese, L., et al. (2010). Recruiting and retaining bilingual interpreters for educational settings: A call for best practices. Communication Disorders Quarterly, 31(4), 209-215.

Reid, G., & Wearmouth, J. (Eds.). (2014). Dyslexia-friendly practice in the secondary classroom. SAGE Publications.

Riddick, B. (2006). Why dyslexic children persistently fail. In G. Reid & J. Wearmouth (Eds.), Dyslexia and literacy: Theory and practice (2nd ed., pp. 165-184). Wiley.

Rumberger, R. W., et al. (2003). Parental involvement in elementary school and educational attainment. Sociology of Education, 76(1), 36-51.

Shaywitz, B. A., et al. (1992). Persistence of dyslexia: The Connecticut Longitudinal Study at adolescence. Pediatrics, 90(4), 592-601.

Shaywitz, S. E. (1998). Dyslexia. New England Journal of Medicine, 338(5), 307-312.

Shaywitz, S. E., et al. (1999). Disruption of posterior brain systems for reading in children with developmental dyslexia. Biological Psychiatry, 45(6), 589-600.

Shaywitz, S. (2003). Overcoming dyslexia: A new and complete science-based program for reading problems at any level. Vintage Books.

Smith, A. E. (2018). Supporting the social-emotional well-being of students with dyslexia. TEACHING Exceptional Children, 50(6),

326-336.

Snowling, M. J., et al. (2003). Longitudinal relations between phonological processing skills and reading in children with reading disabilities. Journal of Child Psychology and Psychiatry, 44(6), 1012-1032.

Snowling, M. J., et al. (2020). Dyslexia: From theory to intervention. Wiley-Blackwell.

Swanson, H. L., & Siegel, L. S. (2001). Learning disabilities as a working memory deficit. Issues in Education, 7(1), 1-48.

Swanson, H. L. (2021). Interventions to Improve Learning, Study Skills, and Reading Comprehension for Students With Learning Disabilities in Secondary School. Journal of Learning Disabilities, 54(1), 27-40.

Turnbull, A. P., et al. (2016). Exceptional lives: Special education in today's schools. Pearson.

Turnbull, A. P., et al. (2021). Families, professionals, and exceptionality: Positive outcomes through partnerships and trust. Routledge.

Wang, M. T., et al. (2020). Classroom context, achievement motivation, and academic engagement: A longitudinal study of Chinese secondary school students. Journal of Educational Psychology, 112(3), 738-753.

Willcutt, E. G., et al. (2010). Understanding comorbidity between specific learning disabilities. New Directions for Child and Adolescent Development, 2010(128), 33-45.

Wolf, M., & Bowers, P. G. (1999). The double-deficit hypothesis for the developmental dyslexias. Journal of Educational Psychology, 91(3), 415-438.

Wren, S. E., et al. (2018). Collaborative partnerships in the identification of specific learning difficulties: A systematic review. Dyslexia, 24(3), 209-227.

CHAPTER THREE
Differentiated Instruction Techniques

Introduction

In today's diverse classrooms, educators face the challenge of meeting the unique needs of every student. Traditional one-size-fits-all instruction may not effectively support the varying learning styles, abilities, and interests of all learners. This is where differentiated instruction comes into play. Differentiated instruction is an instructional approach that acknowledges and responds to the individual strengths, needs, and interests of students. It recognises that learners have different ways of processing information, acquiring skills, and demonstrating understanding. By tailoring instruction to meet these diverse needs, differentiated instruction aims to maximise student engagement and achievement.

The purpose of this chapter is to provide educators with practical techniques and strategies for implementing differentiated instruction in their classrooms. We will explore a range of approaches that can be utilised to differentiate instruction, such as tiered assignments, flexible grouping, learning contracts, curriculum compacting, and the principles of Universal Design for Learning (UDL). These techniques can be applied across content areas, including literacy and language, mathematics, science, and social studies, ensuring that all students have equitable access to the curriculum.

Understanding that implementing differentiated instruction requires thoughtful planning and ongoing assessment, this chapter will also delve into pre-assessment techniques to identify student needs, strategies for assessing and monitoring progress, and the use of formative assessment to guide instruction. Additionally, we will address common challenges and potential pitfalls that educators may encounter when implementing differentiated instruction and discuss ways to overcome them.

It is important to note that differentiated instruction is not about creating separate lesson plans for each student. Rather, it involves providing multiple pathways for students to access and engage with the content, process information, and demonstrate their learning. By adopting differentiated instruction techniques, educators can create inclusive and responsive learning environments that empower students to reach their full potential.

Throughout this chapter, we will emphasise the significance of ongoing reflection and professional development in refining differentiated instruction practices. As educators, our goal is to continually enhance our ability to meet the diverse needs of our students and promote success.

By embracing differentiated instruction, educators can foster a classroom environment that celebrates and supports the unique strengths and abilities of every learner. Let us embark on this journey together and explore the powerful impact that differentiated instruction can have on student engagement, motivation, and achievement.

Understanding Differentiated Instruction

Differentiated instruction is an instructional approach that recognises and addresses the diverse learning needs of students. It is rooted in the belief that every learner is unique, with varying abilities, interests, and readiness levels. Rather than using a one-size-fits-all approach, differentiated instruction acknowledges that students require different pathways and supports to effectively engage with the curriculum and demonstrate their understanding. This section provides an in-depth understanding of differentiated instruction, including its definition, guiding principles, and the benefits it offers to both teachers and students.

Definition of Differentiated Instruction

◎ Differentiated instruction refers to the deliberate planning and implementation of instructional strategies that address the individual learning needs of students (Tomlinson, 2017).

◎ It involves adjusting content, process, and product to suit students' readiness levels, interests, and learning profiles, with the goal of optimising student learning and success (Tomlinson & Moon, 2013).

Principles of Differentiated Instruction

◎ Respect for Student Differences
   o Differentiated instruction recognises and values the diverse abilities, backgrounds, and experiences that students bring to the classroom.

◎ Flexible Instructional Strategies
   o It emphasises the use of varied instructional approaches, materials, and assessments to accommodate different learning styles and preferences.

◎ High Expectations of all Students
   o Differentiated instruction sets high expectations for all learners, believing that each student can achieve academic success with appropriate support and guidance.

◎ Ongoing Assessment and Adjustment
   o It involves continuous assessment of student progress to inform instructional decisions and adjust teaching strategies to meet individual needs.

Benefits of Differentiated Instruction

◎ Improved Student Engagement
   o By tailoring instruction to students' interests and learning styles, differentiated instruction increases student engagement and motivation to learn (Tomlinson, 2014).

◎ Enhanced Academic Achievement

    o When instruction is personalised and responsive to students' individual needs, it promotes deeper understanding and mastery of content (Tomlinson, 2017).

◎ Increased Self-Efficacy and Confidence

    o Differentiated instruction nurtures students' self-belief and confidence by providing opportunities for success and growth based on their abilities and readiness levels (Wormeli, 2017).

◎ Inclusion and Equity

    o It supports an inclusive classroom environment by valuing and accommodating diverse learners, promoting equity in access to education (Tomlinson, 2017).

Differentiated instruction is a dynamic and flexible approach that recognises the diverse learning needs of students. By implementing differentiated instruction, educators can create learning environments that foster engagement, empower students to take ownership of their learning, and promote equitable access to education for all learners.

Preparing for Differentiated Instruction

Preparing for differentiated instruction is a crucial step in ensuring its effective implementation. It involves understanding the diverse needs of students, assessing their readiness levels, and considering cultural and linguistic diversity. This section explores the key aspects of preparing for differentiated instruction, providing educators with practical strategies to create a supportive learning environment that meets the individual needs of all learners.

Assessing Students Needs and Readiness

◎ Formative Assessments

    o Utilise formative assessment strategies, such as diagnostic assessments, observations, and informal checks for understanding, to gather information about students' strengths, challenges, and prior knowledge

(Harlen, 2019).
- Learning Style Inventories
  - Administer learning style inventories to help identify students' preferred ways of learning, such as visual, auditory, or kinaesthetic (Honey & Mumford, 1982).
- Differentiating by Interest
  - Gather information about students' interests and incorporate their preferences into the instructional planning process (Kearney, 2010).

Analysing Learning Profiles and Preferences
- Multiple Intelligence Theory
  - Consider Howard Gardner's theory of multiple intelligences, which suggests that students have diverse strengths and intelligences (Gardner, 1983). Plan activities that align with different intelligences, such as linguistic, logical-mathematical, spatial, bodily-kinaesthetic, musical, interpersonal, intrapersonal, and naturalistic.
- Learning Preferences
  - Recognise that students may have different learning preferences, such as working independently, in small groups, or through hands-on activities. Offer various instructional strategies and opportunities for students to engage with content in ways that suit their preferences (Pashler et al., 2009).

Considering Cultural and Linguistic Diversity
- Culturally Responsive Teaching
  - Embrace culturally responsive teaching practices that honour and incorporate students' diverse cultural backgrounds into the learning experience (Gay, 2018).
- English as an Additional Language (EAL) Learners
  - Provide additional support for students who are learning English as an additional language, including scaffolding instructional materials, using visuals, and providing bilingual resources (Lucas & Villegas, 2011).
- Inclusive Classroom Environment

oFoster an inclusive classroom environment where all students feel valued and respected, regardless of their cultural or linguistic backgrounds (Ofsted, 2019).

By understanding students' needs, readiness levels, and preferences, educators can better tailor instruction to meet the diverse learning requirements of their students. The preparation phase lays the foundation for effective differentiation, ensuring that instruction is engaging, relevant, and accessible to all learners in the classroom.

Strategies for Differentiated Instruction

Implementing differentiated instruction involves employing a range of strategies that cater to the diverse learning needs, readiness levels, and interests of students. This section explores various practical techniques that educators can utilise to differentiate instruction effectively and create inclusive learning environments.

Tiered Assignments and Tasks
- Develop Tied assignments that provide multiple levels of complexity, allowing students to engage with the content at their readiness level (Tomlinson, 2017).
- Vary the difficulty or complexity of tasks, offering different entry points and levels of challenge based on students' abilities (Gregory & Chapman, 2007).
- Provide scaffolding or support for struggling students while offering extensions or enrichment activities for advanced learners (Tomlinson & Moon, 2013).

Flexible Grouping and Cooperative Learning
- Group students strategically based on their learning needs, strengths, or interests, fostering collaboration and peer support (Kagan, 2009).
- Utilise cooperative learning structures, such as jigsaws, think-pair-share, or reciprocal teaching, to encourage active engagement and participation (Slavin, 1995).
- Implement stations or learning centres where students rotate through different activities or tasks to address various learning

objectives or modalities (Tomlinson, 2014).

Learning Contracts and Choice Boards

- ◎ Offer learning contracts that outline individualised goals, expectations, and choices for students to demonstrate their understanding (Tomlinson & Moon, 2013).
- ◎ Use choice boards or menus that present a variety of options for students to select activities or assignments aligned with their interests and learning preferences (Brody & Alleman, 2016).
- ◎ Incorporate student voice and input into the creation of learning contracts or choice boards, allowing them to have ownership of their learning experiences (McCarthy, 2015).

Curriculum Compacting and Acceleration

- ◎ Assess students' prior knowledge and skills to identify areas of mastery. Compact the curriculum by allowing advanced learners to move through content more quickly (Reis et al., 1995).
- ◎ Provide opportunities for students to delve deeper into topics of interest or pursue independent projects that extend beyond the standard curriculum (Tomlinson, 2017).
- ◎ Offer acceleration options, such as advanced coursework or enrichment opportunities, to challenge high-achieving students (VanTassel-Baska et al., 2004).

Universal Design for Learning (UDL) Principles

- ◎ Incorporate UDL principles to provide multiple means of representation, engagement, and expression to accommodate diverse learners (CAST, 2018).
- ◎ Offer multimodal materials and resources, including visuals, audio recordings, and interactive digital tools, to support different learning styles (Rose & Meyer, 2002).
- ◎ Provide options for student engagement, such as offering varied choices for assignments or allowing students to demonstrate understanding through different modes (Hall et al., 2012).

By employing these strategies, educators can differentiate instruction effectively and create inclusive learning environments where all students can engage, participate, and thrive.

Differentiating Instruction Across Content Areas

Differentiating instruction across content areas is essential to meet the diverse learning needs of students in various subject domains. Different content areas require different approaches to instruction, and this section explores practical strategies for differentiating instruction in literacy, mathematics, science, and social studies.

Differentiating Instruction in Literacy
- Varied Reading Materials
  - Provide a range of reading materials at different reading levels, allowing students to access texts that match their reading abilities (Tomlinson & Moon, 2013).
- Graphic Organisers and Visual Aids
  - Use graphic organisers and visual aids to support comprehension and organisation of information, accommodating different learning styles (Vacca et al., 2019).
- Scaffolding Writing Tasks
  - Offer scaffolding supports, such as graphic organisers, sentence starters, or peer collaboration, to assist students in planning, drafting, and revising their written work (Tomlinson, 2014).

Differentiating Instruction in Mathematics
- Flexible Grouping for Maths Tasks
  - Group students based on their readiness levels or specific maths skills, allowing for targeted instruction and practice (Tomlinson & Moon, 2013).
- Manipulatives and Visual Representations
  - Incorporate manipulatives, models, and visual representations to support conceptual understanding

and problem-solving in mathematics (Briars & Resnick, 2004).
- ◎ Choice of Maths Tasks
    - oProvide students with a choice of maths tasks or problem-solving activities, allowing them to select tasks that align with their interests or learning preferences (Tomlinson, 2017).

Differentiating Instruction in Science
- ◎ Varied Learning Experiences
    - oOffer a variety of learning experiences, such as hands-on experiments, multimedia resources, virtual simulations, or outdoor investigations, to cater to different learning preferences (Bybee, 2009).
- ◎ Multiple Entry Points
    - oDesign science tasks with multiple entry points, allowing students to engage with the content at different levels of complexity and depth (Tomlinson, 2014).
- ◎ Differentiated Assessments
    - oProvide varied assessment options, including written reflections, oral presentations, or hands-on demonstrations, to allow students to demonstrate their understanding in different ways (Wiggins & McTighe, 2005).

Differentiating Instruction in Social Studies
- ◎ Choice-Based Projects
    - oAssign open-ended projects or research tasks that allow students to choose topics aligned with their interests or cultural backgrounds (Fogarty & Pete, 2008).
- ◎ Simulations and Role-Playing
    - oEngage students in simulations or role-playing activities to enhance their understanding of historical events or social issues (VanSledright, 2002).
- ◎ Multimedia Resources
    - oIncorporate multimedia resources, primary source documents, and diverse perspectives to provide a comprehensive view of social studies topics (National

Council for the Social Studies, 2013).

By differentiating instruction across content areas, educators can create engaging learning experiences that address students' unique learning needs and promote meaningful understanding in specific subject domains.

Assessing and Monitoring Student Progress

Assessing and monitoring student progress is a crucial aspect of differentiated instruction. It allows educators to gather valuable data about students' learning, making informed instructional decisions, and adjust teaching strategies to meet individual needs. This section explores effective strategies for assessing and monitoring student progress in the context of differentiated instructions.

Formative Assessment Strategies for Differentiation

- Ongoing Checks for Understanding
  - o Use a variety of formative assessment techniques, such as exit tickets, quick quizzes, or class discussions, to gauge student understanding and identify areas of strength and challenge (Black & William, 1998).
- Observations and Anecdotal Records
  - o Make systematic observations of students' participation, engagement, and progress during classroom activities and document these observations in anecdotal records (Marzano et al., 2003).
- Learning Conferences and Self-Reflections
  - o Engage students in one-on-one conferences or self-reflection activities to assess their understanding, reflect on their learning progress, and set goals (Hattie & Timperley, 2007).

Tracking Student Growth and Adjusting Instruction

- Student Portfolios
  - o Use student portfolios to collect and showcase evidence of learning, including samples of student work,

self-reflections, and goal-setting (Tomlinson & Moon, 2013).

- ◉ Learning Progression and Rubrics
    - oDevelop learning progressions or rubrics that outline expected learning outcomes and criteria for proficiency, allowing students to track their growth and understand expectations (Heritage, 2010).
- ◉ Data-Drive Instruction
    - oAnalyse assessment data, such as quizzes, texts, or performance tasks, to identify patterns and trends, and use this information to inform instructional decisions and adjust teaching strategies (DuFour et al., 2016).

Providing Feedback and Promoting Self-Assessment

- ◉ Timely and Specific Feedback
    - oProvide constructive feedback that is timely, specific, and actionable, focusing on areas of strength and suggestions for improvement (Hattie & Timperley, 2007)
- ◉ Peer Feedback and Collaboration
    - oEncourage peer feedback and collaborative learning opportunities, where students provide feedback to one another, fostering a culture of constructive critique and growth (Van der Kleij et al., 2015).
- ◉ Self-Assessment and Goal-Setting
    - oPromote self-assessment by encouraging students to reflect on their own learning progress, set goals, and monitor their growth towards those goals (Brookhart, 2013).

Using Data to Inform Instructional Decisions

- ◉ Differentiated Groups and Interventions
    - oAnalyse assessment data to identify students' specific learning needs and group them accordingly, offering targeted interventions or enrichment opportunities (Tomlinson, 2017).
- ◉ Adjusting Instructional Strategies
    - oUse assessment data to identify areas where instructional

adjustments are needed, such as modifying the pace, depth, or complexity of instruction to better meet students' needs (Hattie, 2012).

◎ Individualised Goal-Setting

oCollaboratively set individualised learning goals with students based on their assessment data, helping them understand their current performance and plan for improvement (William, 2011).

By employing effective assessment and monitoring strategies, educators can gather valuable insights into students' progress, adapt instruction accordingly, and provide timely support to ensure continued growth and success in differentiated classrooms.

Addressing Common Challenges and Potential Pitfalls

Implementing differentiated instruction may come with its fair share of challenges and potential pitfalls. It is important for educators to be aware of these challenges and have strategies in place to address them effectively. This section explores common challenges that educators may encounter in implementing differentiated instruction and provides practical solutions to over them.

Overcoming Time Constraints and Workload Challenges

One of the primary challenges in implementing differentiated instruction is managing the additional time and workload required for planning and delivering personalised instruction. To address this challenge, educators can:

◎ Collaborative with colleagues to share resources, ideas, and responsibilities (Tomlinson, 2017).

◎ Leverage technology tools and resources to streamline administrative tasks and create personalised learning experiences (Brookhart & Spencer, 2016).

◎ Prioritise instructional goals and focus on essential content, ensuring a balance between differentiation and effective time management (Tomlinson & Moon, 2013).

Addressing Resistance to Change and Scepticism

Resistance to change or scepticism from colleagues, senior management, or even students' parents can present obstacles to implementing differentiated instruction. To address this challenge, educators can:

- ◎ Engage in open and honest communication with stakeholders, sharing research, evidence, and success stories of differentiated instruction (Tomlinson, 2017).
- ◎ Provide professional development opportunities to build understanding and capacity for differentiated instruction among educators (Gregory & Chapman, 2007).
- ◎ Offer clear explanations of the rationale and benefits of differentiated instruction, emphasising its positive impact on student learning and achievement (Tomlinson & Moon, 2013).

Promoting Inclusivity and Equity in Differentiated Instruction

Ensuring that differentiated instruction is inclusive and equitable for all students can be a challenge. To address this, educators can:

- ◎ Regularly reflect on their instructional practices to identify potential biases and ensure equitable access to learning opportunities for all students (Ford et al., 2017).
- ◎ Incorporate culturally responsive teaching practices that honour and value students' diverse backgrounds and experiences (Gay, 2018).
- ◎ Provide ongoing support and accommodations for students with special educational needs or disabilities, ensuring their inclusion in differentiated instruction (Tomlinson & Moon, 2013).

Professional Development and Collaboration for Effective Differentiation

Building expertise in differentiated instruction and fostering collaboration among educators are essential for successful implementation. To address this, educators can:

- ◎ Engage in professional development opportunities that focus on differentiated instruction techniques and strategies (Tomlinson, 2014).
- ◎ Create professional learning communities or networks where educators can share best practices, resources, and support one

another in implementing differentiated instruction (DuFour et al., 2016).

⊚ Foster a culture of continuous improvement, encouraging educators to reflect on their practice and seek feedback from colleagues (Tomlinson & Moon, 2013).

By addressing these common challenges and potential pitfalls, educators can create a supportive environment that promotes effective differentiated instruction and ensures meaningful learning experiences for all students.

Conclusion

In conclusion, differentiated instruction is a powerful approach that recognises and addresses the diverse learning needs of students. By tailoring instruction to accommodate variations in readiness levels, interests, and learning profiles, educators can create inclusive and engaging learning environments that promote academic growth and success for all students. Throughout this chapter, we have explored the foundations of differentiated instruction, including its definition, guiding principles, and the benefits it offers. We have discussed strategies for preparing, implementing, and assessing differentiated instruction, as well as addressed common challenges and potential pitfalls that educators may encounter. By applying the principles and strategies discussed in this chapter, educators can create a supportive classroom environment that empowers students, promotes their individual growth, and fosters a love for learning. Differentiated instruction provides the framework for educators to meet the diverse needs of their students and ensure equitable access to high-quality education. As educators continue to explore and refine their practice in differentiated instruction, they contribute to the creation of inclusive, engaging, and empowering learning experiences that support the success of every student.

References

Black, P., & Wiliam, D. (1998). Inside the black box: Raising standards through classroom assessment. Phi Delta Kappan, 80(2), 139-148.

Briars, D. J., & Resnick, L. B. (2004). Standards-based mathematics assessment in the classroom. NCTM.

Brody, L. E., & Alleman, J. (2016). Differentiating instruction in a whole-group setting: Taking the easy first step. Gifted Child Today, 39(4), 223-230.

Brookhart, S. M. (2013). How to assess higher-order thinking skills in your classroom. ASCD.

Brookhart, S. M., & Spencer, K. (2016). Assessment for learning in the differentiated classroom. ASCD.

Bybee, R. W. (2009). The BSCS 5E instructional model and 21st-century skills. The Science Teacher, 76(8), 43-49.

CAST. (2018). Universal Design for Learning guidelines version 2.2. Retrieved from http://udlguidelines.cast.org

DuFour, R., et al. (2016). Learning by doing: A handbook for professional learning communities at work (3rd ed.). Solution Tree.

Fogarty, R., & Pete, B. M. (2008). Differentiating instruction for English learners: Making content accessible. Corwin Press.

Ford, D. Y., et al. (2017). Culturally responsive classrooms for culturally diverse students with and at risk of disabilities. Review of Research in Education, 41(1), 235-267.

Gay, G. (2018). Culturally responsive teaching: Theory, research, and practice (3rd ed.). Teachers College Press.

Gardner, H. (1983). Frames of mind: The theory of multiple intelligences. Basic Books.

Gregory, G. H., & Chapman, C. (2007). Differentiated instructional strategies: One size doesn't fit all. Corwin Press.

Hall, T., et al. (2012). Universal design for learning in the classroom: Practical applications. Guilford Press.

Harlen, W. (2019). Teaching and learning primary science. Routledge.

Hattie, J. (2012). Visible learning for teachers: Maximizing impact on learning. Routledge.

Hattie, J., & Timperley, H. (2007). The power of feedback. Review of Educational Research, 77(1), 81-112.

Heritage, M. (2010). Formative assessment: Making it happen in the classroom. Corwin Press.

Honey, P., & Mumford, A. (1982). The manual of learning styles. Peter Honey Publications.

Kagan, S. (2009). Kagan cooperative learning. Kagan Publishing.

Kearney, M. (2010). An investigation into the effects of learning styles on student learning outcomes. Irish Journal of Academic Practice, 1(1), 1-22.

Lucas, T., & Villegas, A. M. (2011). Preparing linguistically responsive teachers: Laying the foundation in preservice teacher education. Theory into Practice, 50(4), 298-305.

Marzano, R. J., et al. (2003). Classroom assessment and grading that work. ASCD.

McCarthy, J. (2015). So each may learn: Integrating learning styles and multiple intelligences. Rowman & Littlefield.

National Council for the Social Studies. (2013). The college, career, and civic life (C3) framework for social studies state standards. Retrieved from https://www.socialstudies.org/sites/default/files/c3/C3-Framework-for-Social-Studies.pdf

Ofsted. (2019). Education inspection framework. Retrieved from https://www.gov.uk/government/publications/education-inspection-framework

Pashler, H., et al. (2009). Learning styles: Concepts and evidence. Psychological Science in the Public Interest, 9(3), 105-119.

Reis, S. M., et al. (1995). Curriculum compacting: The complete guide to modifying the regular curriculum for high ability students. Prufrock Press.

Rose, D. H., & Meyer, A. (2002). Teaching every student in the digital age: Universal design for learning. ASCD.

Slavin, R. E. (1995). Cooperative learning: Theory, research, and practice (2nd ed.). Allyn & Bacon.

Tomlinson, C. A. (2014). The differentiated classroom: Responding to the needs of all learners (2nd ed.). ASCD.

Tomlinson, C. A. (2017). How to differentiate instruction in academically diverse classrooms (3rd ed.). ASCD.

Tomlinson, C. A., & Moon, T. R. (2013). Assessment and student success in a differentiated classroom. ASCD.

Vacca, R. T., et al. (2019). Content area reading: Literacy and learning across the curriculum (12th ed.). Pearson.

VanSledright, B. A. (2002). In search of America's past: Learning to read history in elementary school. Teachers College Press.

VanTassel-Baska, J., et al. (2004). Comprehensive curriculum for gifted learners (3rd ed.). Corwin Press.

Van der Kleij, F. M., et al. (2015). The effect of feedback in computer-based assessment for learning: A meta-analysis. Review of Educational Research, 85(4), 475-511.

Wiggins, G. P., & McTighe, J. (2005). Understanding by design (2nd ed.). ASCD.

Wiliam, D. (2011). Embedded formative assessment. Solution Tree.

Wormeli, R. (2017). Fair isn't always equal: Assessing and grading in the differentiated classroom (2nd ed.). Stenhouse Publishers.

CHAPTER FOUR

Reading and Literacy Strategies

Introduction

The ability to read and comprehend written text is a fundamental skill that opens door to knowledge, self-expression, and academic success. However, for dyslexic learners, reading can be a challenging and frustrating experience. Dyslexia is a neurodevelopmental disorder that affects the acquisition of reading skills, making it crucial for educators to understand and implement effective strategies to support these students in their reading and literacy development. This chapter will explore a range of evidence-based strategies and approaches specifically designed to address the unique needs of dyslexia learners. By implementing these strategies, educators can create an inclusive and supportive learning environment that empowers dyslexia learners to develop their reading skills, enhance their literacy abilities, and foster a lifelong love for reading. Through the exploration of phonological awareness, reading comprehension strategies, vocabulary development, fluency building, assistive technology, accommodations, and more, this chapter aims to equip educators with practical tools to effectively support dyslexic learners on their journey towards reading proficiency and literacy achievement.

Understanding Dyslexia and Reading Difficulties

Dyslexia is a neurodevelopmental disorder that significantly impacts reading and related language skills. It is characterised by difficulties in accurate and fluent word recognition, poor spelling, and decoding abilities (Lyon et al., 2003). Understanding the nature of dyslexia and the specific reading difficulties experienced by dyslexic learners is crucial for educators to provide effective support.

Definition and Types of Dyslexia

Dyslexia is a complex condition with variations in its presentation and severity. It is important to note that dyslexia is not indicative of intelligence or overall cognitive ability. There are different subtypes of dyslexia, including phonological dyslexia (difficulties in phonological progressing), surface dyslexia (difficulties with irregular word reading), and mixed dyslexia (a combination of phonological and surface dyslexia) (Shaywitz & Shaywitz, 2008).

Phonological Processing Difficulties

Phonological processing refers to the ability to manipulate and analyse the sounds of spoken language. Dyslexic learners often struggle with phonological awareness, which includes tasks such as segmenting, blending, and manipulating sounds. These difficulties can impede their ability to decode and spell words (Snowling & Hulme, 2012).

Working Memory Challenges

Dyslexic learners frequently exhibit working memory limitations, which can impact their ability to hold and manipulate information during reading tasks. This can result in difficulties with remembering and applying phonics rules, recognising sight words, and comprehending texts (Swanson, 2003).

Visual and Orthographic Processing Differences

Dyslexic learners may also experience challenges with visual and orthographic processing, which affect their ability to recognise and differentiate letters, words, and visual patterns. Difficulties in visual processing can hinder accurate word recognition and lead to letter reversals or visual confusions (Vidyasagar & Pammer, 2010).

Understanding these core aspects of dyslexia and the associated reading difficulties provides educators with insights into the specific challenges faced by dyslexic learners. By addressing these difficulties through targeted instructional strategies, educators can support dyslexic learners in developing their reading skills and overcoming the barriers they encounter.

Phonological Awareness and Phonics Instruction

Phonological awareness and phonics instruction play a crucial role in supporting dyslexic learners in developing strong reading skills. Phonological awareness refers to the ability to recognise and manipulate the sounds of language, including individual phonemes, syllables, and rhymes. Phonics instruction, on the other hand, focuses on teaching the relationships between sounds and written letters or letter patterns (Ehri et al., 2001). This section explores effective strategies to enhance phonological awareness and provide explicit phonics instruction for dyslexic learners.

Developing Phonological Awareness Skills
Dyslexic learners often struggle with phonological awareness, making it essential to provide explicit instruction and practice in this area. Effective strategies include:

- ◎ Phonemic Awareness Activities – *engage students in activities that focus on segmenting, blending, and manipulating individual phonemes. This can include tasks such as phoneme segmentation, sound blending, and phoneme substitution (Torgese et al., 2001).*
- ◎ Syllable and Rhyme Awareness – *encourage students to identify and manipulate syllables and recognise rhyming words. Activities such as clapping syllables or playing rhyming word games can be beneficial (Ehri et al., 2001).*
- ◎ Word Awareness – *help students develop an understanding of*

words as units of sound by emphasising syllable and onset-rime segmentation. This can involve breaking words into syllables or identifying common word patterns (Snow et al., 1998).

Explicit Phonics Instruction

Explicit phonic instruction provides dyslexic learners with systematic and structured instruction on letter-sound relationships. Effective strategies for phonics instruction include:

- Synthetic Phonics Approach – *teach letter-sound correspondence in isolation and then blend them to form words. This involves explicitly teaching the sounds associated with individual letters or letter groups (National Reading Panel, 2000).*

- Multisensory Techniques – *incorporate multisensory activities that engage multiple senses, such as using manipulatives, tracing letters while saying the sounds, or incorporating movement into phonics lessons. This approach helps reinforce learning through different modalities (Orton, 1937).*

- Decoding Strategies – *teacher decoding strategies to support dyslexic learners in applying phonics skills to unfamiliar words. Strategies may include sounding out, chunking, or using context clues to aid word recognition (Ehri et al., 2001).*

By providing explicit instruction in phonological awareness and phonics, educators can support dyslexic learners in developing strong foundational reading skills. These skills serve as building blocks for accurate decoding, word recognition, and spelling, helping dyslexic learners become more confident and proficient readers.

Reading Comprehension Strategies

Reading comprehension is a critical component of literacy, and dyslexic learners often face challenges in this area. Implementing effective reading comprehension strategies can support dyslexic learners in understanding and interpreting texts more effectively. This section explores strategies to enhance reading comprehension for dyslexic learners.

Activating Prior Knowledge

Activating prior knowledge helps dyslexic learners make connections between their existing knowledge and the new information they encounter in texts.

Strategies to activate prior knowledge include:

◉ Pre-Reading Activities – *engage students in discussions, brainstorming, or concept mapping related to the topic or theme of the text. This helps activate relevant background knowledge and build anticipation for reading (Duke & Pearson, 2002).*

◉ KWL Charts – *Use KWL (Know - Want to Know - Learned) charters or similar graphic organisers to help students identify what they already know, what they want to learn, and what they have learned after reading. This promotes active engagement with the text and meta-cognitive thinking (Ogle, 1986).*

Text Structure Awareness

Dyslexic learners can benefit from explicit instruction on text structures, which help them organise and comprehend information within a text.

Strategies for developing text structure awareness include:

◉ Graphic Organisers – *utilise graphic organisers, such as story maps or concept maps, to visually represent the organisation and relationships within a text. This helps dyslexic learners visualise and understand the structure of the information (Dole et al., 1991).*

◉ Text Structure Instruction – *teach students different text structures, such as cause and effect, compare and contrast, or problem and solution. Explicitly point out signal words or phrases that indicate specific text structures (Vacca et al., 2014).*

Questioning Techniques

Encouraging dyslexic learners to ask questions before, during, and after reading supports their engagement with the text and promotes deeper comprehension.

Strategies for effective questioning include:

◉ Questioning Stems – *provide students with question prompts or stems that guide their thinking while reading. This helps dyslexic learners focus on key ideas, make connections, and monitor their understanding (Gambrell & Koskinen, 2003).*

◉ Collaborative Questioning – *engage students in small group or whole-class discussions where they can ask and respond to questions*

related to the text. This promotes active participation and a deeper
understanding of the material (Rosenshine & Meister, 1994).

Meta-cognitive Strategies

Meta-cognition involves thinking about one's thinking and is essential for dyslexic learners to monitor their comprehension and adjust their reading strategies.

Strategies to promote meta-cognitive skills include:

- Think-Alouds – *model the thinking process by verbalising thoughts while reading. This helps dyslexic learners develop awareness of comprehension strategies, such as making predictions, clarifying confusion, or summarising (Pressley & Afflerbach, 1995).*

- Self-Questioning – *encouraging students to ask themselves questions while reading and reflect on their understanding. This internal dialogue enhances metacognitive awareness and helps dyslexic learners monitor their comprehension (Baker & Brown, 1984).*

By implementing these reading comprehension strategies, educators can empower dyslexic learners to become active and engaged readers, enhancing their comprehension skills, and fostering a deeper understanding of texts.

Vocabulary Development

Developing a robust vocabulary is crucial for dyslexic learners to enhance their reading comprehension and overall language skills. Effective vocabulary development strategies can help dyslexic learners expand their word knowledge, improve word recognition, and deepen their understanding of texts. This section explores strategies to support vocabulary development in dyslexic learners.

Explicit Vocabulary Instruction

Dyslexic learners benefit from explicit instruction that focuses on teaching word meanings and connections.

Strategies for explicit vocabulary instruction include:

- Selecting Target Words – *identify important words or vocabulary terms that are essential for understanding the text. Prioritise words that are critical for comprehension and recurring in academic contexts (Beck et al., 2002).*

- ◎ Contextual and Visual Cues – *teacher students to use contextual clues, such as surrounding words or phrases, to infer word meanings. Utilise visual aids, such as pictures, diagrams, or graphic organisers, to support understanding (Marzano et al., 2001).*
- ◎ Word Exploration Activities – *engage dyslexic learners in activities that promote word exploration, such as defining words in the own words, creating semantic maps, or generating examples and non-examples (Graves, 2006).*

Word-Learning Strategies

Dyslexic learners can benefit from explicit instruction in effective word-learning strategies.

Strategies to enhance word learning include:

- ◎ Morphological Analysis – *teach students to identify and analyse meaningful word parts, such as prefixes, suffixes, and root words. This helps dyslexic learners decode and understand unfamiliar words (Goodwin & Ahn, 2010).*
- ◎ Dictionary and Digital Tools – *encourage dyslexic learners to use dictionaries or digital tools to look up word meanings and explore word usage. Teach them how to effectively use these resources to enhance vocabulary development (Nagy et al., 2005).*
- ◎ Word Associations and Connections – *help students make connections between new words and their prior knowledge. Encourage them to create associations, relate new words to known concepts, or make connections through analogies (Baumann et al., 2003).*

Vocabulary in Context

Exposing dyslexic learners to rich and meaningful language contexts can enhance their vocabulary development.

Strategies to promote vocabulary in context include:

- ◎ Wide Reading Experiences – *encourage dyslexic learners to engage in extensive reading across various genres and topics. This exposure to diverse texts exposes them to new vocabulary and improves word usage (Nagy & Anderson, 1984).*

- Sustained Oral Language Interactions – *provide opportunities for dyslexic learners to engage in meaningful conversations and discussions. This oral language development supports vocabulary growth through exposure to new words and models of usage (Beck et al., 2002).*

By implementing these vocabulary development strategies, educators can support dyslexic learners in building a strong word knowledge base, improving their reading comprehension, and enhancing their overall language proficiency.

Fluency Development

Developing fluency is a critical aspect of reading proficiency for dyslexic learners. Fluency encompasses the ability to read with accuracy, speed, and expression, leading to better comprehension and overall reading enjoyment. This section explores strategies to enhance fluency development in dyslexic learners.

Model and Provide Guided Reading Practice

Dyslexic learners benefit from modelled fluent reading and guided practice.

Strategies for modelling and guided reading practice include:

- Teacher Modelling – *demonstrate fluent reading by reading aloud to the class, emphasising expression, phrasing, and smooth pacing. This provides dyslexic learners with a model of fluent reading (Rasinski, 2011).*
- Paired Reading – *engage dyslexic learners in paired reading activities where they read with a more fluent partner, such as a teacher or a peer. This provides support, builds confidence, and promotes the development of reading fluency (Fuchs et al., 2001).*

Repeated Reading and Timed Reading

Repeated reading exercises can help dyslexic learners improve reading fluency by increasing their speed and automaticity.

Strategies for repeated reading and timed reading include:

- Choral Reading – *encourage dyslexic learners to read aloud in unison with their peers or the teacher. This provides opportunities for repeated reading and helps develop pacing and rhythm (Kuhn et al., 2010).*

◎ Timed Reading – *use timed reading activities where dyslexic learners read a passage multiple times, aiming to improve their reading speed and accuracy with each reading. This helps develop automaticity and fluency (Raninski et al., 2005).*

Audio-Assisted Reading

Utilising audio-assisted reading techniques can support dyslexic learners in developing fluency and comprehension.

Strategies for audio-assisted reading include:

◎ Audiobooks or Text-to-Speech Software – *provide dyslexic learners with access to audiobooks or text-to-speech software that highlights the text while it is being read aloud. This helps dyslexic learners follow along and develop a sense of fluency (Heim et al., 2015).*

◎ Echo Reading – *have dyslexic learners listen to a fluent reader and read the same text aloud, imitating the model's pace, phrasing, and expression. This assists dyslexic learners in developing their own fluency (Therrien et al., 2006).*

Phrased and Expressive Reading

Dyslexic learners can benefit from practicing reading in meaningful phrases and incorporating expression into their reading.

Strategies for phrased and expressive reading include:

◎ Phrased Reading – *encourage dyslexic learners to group words together in meaningful phrases rather than reading word by word. This helps develop natural phrasing and smoother reading (Rasinski, 2011).*

◎ Reader's Theatre – *engage dyslexic learners in reader's theatre activities where they read scripts or passages with expression, emphasising character voices and emotions. This promotes fluency and expressive reading (McKool et al., 2010).*

By implementing these fluency development strategies, educators can support dyslexic learners in developing their reading fluency, enhancing their reading enjoyment, and improving overall comprehension.

Assistive Technology and Accommodations

Assistive technology and accommodations tailored to reading and significantly support dyslexic learners in accessing and comprehending text more effectively. These tools and strategies provide essential support and foster inclusive learning environments. This section explores various assistive technology options and accommodations specifically designed to enhance reading for dyslexic learners.

Assistive Technology Tools for Reading

Assistive technology offers a range of tools that can enhance reading experiences for dyslexic learners.

Examples of assistive technology tools for reading include:

- ◎ Text-to-Speech Software – *utilise software that converts written text into spoken words, allowing dyslexic learners to listen to text while following along (Higgins & Raskind, 2005).*
- ◎ E-Book Readers and Digital Text – *provide dyslexic learners with access to e-books or digital text, which often offer features like adjustable fonts, text highlighting, and customisable backgrounds (Gentry et al., 2013).*
- ◎ Reading Apps and Browser Extensions – *introduce dyslexic learners to specialised reading apps or browser extensions that provide features like text-to-speech, word highlighting, and dictionary support (Ehri et al., 2021).*

Accommodations for Reading

Implementing accommodations specifically designed for reading can help dyslexic learners access and comprehend text more effectively.

Accommodations my include:

- ◎ Extended Time – *provide dyslexic learners with additional time for reading tasks, assignments, or assessments, considering the extra processing time they may require (Shaywitz et al., 2007).*
- ◎ Preferential Seating – *allow dyslexic learners to choose seating*

positions that minimise distractions and optimise their visual access to the text and instructional materials (Hutchinson et al., 2003).

◎ Text Customisation – *adjust the formatting of texts to meet the specific needs of dyslexic learners, such as using larger fonts, increased line spacing, or alternative colour schemes (Vanderwood et al., 2012).*

◎ Use of Reading Guides – *utilise reading guides, such as window overlays or ruler-like tools, to help dyslexic learners focus on individual lines of text and reduce visual distractions (Pumfrey & Reason, 2001).*

Audiobooks and Read-Aloud Support

Audiobooks and read-aloud support can significantly benefit dyslexic learners by providing access to the content while reducing reading barriers.

Strategies for audiobooks and read-aloud support include:

◎ Audiobooks – *provide dyslexic learners with access to audiobooks, either in digital or physical formats, allowing them to listen to the text being read aloud (Blackhurst et al., 2011).*

◎ Peer or Teacher Reading – *arrange for dyslexic learners to have opportunities to listen to peers or teachers read aloud texts, providing additional support and modelling fluent reading (Rasinski et al., 2005).*

Scaffolded Reading and Guided Support

Scaffolded reading approaches and guided support can assist dyslexic learners in navigating challenging texts.

Strategies for scaffolded reading and guided support include:

◎ Pre-Reading Activities – *engage dyslexic learners in pre-reading activities that activate prior knowledge, set reading purposes, and build interest in the topic or content (Duke & Pearson, 2002).*

◎ Guided Reading Groups – *organise small-group guided reading sessions where dyslexic learners receive targeted support, practice reading strategies, and discuss the text collaboratively (Fountas & Pinnell, 2017).*

◎ Reading Comprehension Strategies – *teach dyslexic learners specific reading comprehension strategies, such as summarising, making predictions, asking questions, and visualising, to support their understanding of the text (Pressley & Afflerback, 1995)*

By implementing assistive technology tools and appropriate accommodations for reading, educators can create inclusive and supportive learning environments that empower dyslexic learners to overcome reading challenges, access educational content, and develop stronger reading skills.

Cultivating a Dyslexia-Friendly Classroom

Creating a dyslexia-friendly classroom environment is essential to support dyslexic learners in their reading developing and overall academic success. A dyslexia-friendly classroom fosters a positive and inclusive atmosphere where reading challenges are acknowledged, and appropriate strategies are implemented to maximise learning opportunities. This section explores key elements for cultivating a dyslexia-friendly classroom.

Awareness and Understanding

Cultivating a dyslexia-friendly classroom begins with raising awareness and promoting understanding among educators and students.

Key strategies include:

- Educator Professional Development – *provide training and professional development opportunities for educators to deepen their understanding of dyslexia, its impact on reading, and effective instructional strategies (Reid et al., 2009).*
- Classroom Discussions – *engage students in age-appropriate discussions about dyslexia, emphasising its strengths and challenges, and promoting empathy and respect among peers (Moats & Dakin, 2008).*

Environmental Considerations

Designing the physical and visual environment of the classroom can create a dyslexia-friendly space that supports reading.

Consider the following:

- Optimal Lighting and Seating – *ensure appropriate lighting and seating arrangements that minimise glare, enhance visual clarity, and provide comfortable reading positions (Hutchinson et al., 2003).*

- ⊚ Print Accessibility – *utilise dyslexia-friendly fonts, clear and legible text, appropriate font size, and adequate spacing in materials, worksheets, and displays to improve readability (Vanderwood et al., 2012).*
- ⊚ Visual Supports – *incorporate visual aids, such as word walls, labelled charts, and visual schedules, to provide additional support for vocabulary development, comprehension, and organisation (Reid et al., 2009).*

Differentiated Instruction

Implementing differentiated instruction ensures that dyslexic learners receive tailored support and appropriate reading instruction.

Strategies for differentiated instruction include:

- ⊚ Multisensory Techniques – *incorporate multisensory approaches, such as Orton-Gillingham based methods, that engage multiple senses (visual, auditory, and kinaesthetic) to reinforce reading skills (Simmons & Kame'enui, 1998).*
- ⊚ Flexible Grouping – *group students based on their reading needs and abilities, allowing for targeted instruction and the provision of additional support to dyslexic learners (Tomlinson & Moon, 2013).*
- ⊚ Individualised Learning Plans – *develop individualised learning plans (IEPs) or personalised education plans (PEPs) that outline specific accommodations, instructional strategies, and goals for dyslexic learners (Graham & Harris, 2005).*

Supportive Classroom Culture

Foster a supportive classroom culture that encourages risk-taking, celebrate effort and progress, and promotes self-advocacy.

Strategies for creating a supportive classroom culture include:

- ⊚ Growth Mindset – *cultivate a growth mindset by promoting the belief that abilities and skills can be developed with effort, perseverance, and effective strategies (Dweck, 2006).*
- ⊚ Encouraging Self-Advocacy – *empower dyslexic learners to advocate for their own reading needs, ask for support when needed, and develop self-awareness of their strengths and challenges (Ehri et al., 2021).*
- ⊚ Positive Feedback and Reinforcement – *provide specific and*

constructive feedback that recognises progress, effort, and
improvement in reading skills, promoting a sense of accomplishment
and motivation (Hattie & Timperley, 2007).

By implementing these strategies and creating a dyslexia-friendly classroom environment, educators can foster a supportive atmosphere that values each student's reading journey, promotes inclusive learning, and maximises the reading potential of dyslexic learners.

Assessment and Progress Monitoring

Assessing and monitoring the progress of dyslexic learners is essential to ensure their reading growth and provide targeted support. This section explores key considerations and strategies for effective assessment and progress monitoring in the context of dyslexia.

Diagnostic Assessments

Diagnostic assessments help identify dyslexic learners and provide a comprehensive understanding of their specific reading strengths and challenges.

Consider the following strategies:

- ◎ Phonological Awareness Assessments – *administer assessments that measure dyslexic learners' abilities to recognise and manipulate sounds in words, as difficulties in phonological awareness are a common characterstic of dyslexia (Hulme & Snowling, 2009).*
- ◎ Decoding and Word Recognition Assessments – *use assessments that assess dyslexic learners' abilities to decode and recognise words accurately and efficiently, identifying areas of weakness and informing targeted interventions (Nation, 2005).*
- ◎ Reading Comprehension Assessments – *include assessments that measure dyslexic learners' comprehension skills, focusing on their ability to understand and make meaning from text (Catts & Kamhi, 2017).*

Progress Monitoring

Regular progress monitoring allows educators to track dyslexic learners' reading growth over time and make data-informed instructional decisions.

Consider the following strategies:

- Curriculum-Based Measurements (CBM) – *implement CBM tools to assess dyslexic learners' reading fluency, accuracy, and comprehension on a regular basis, providing real-time data on progress and areas that require further support (Fuchs & Fuchs, 2006).*
- Informal Reading Inventories (IRIs) – *utilise IRIs to assess dyslexic learners' reading skills, including word recognition, fluency, and comprehension, to monitor progress and adjust instruction accordingly (Johns, 2017).*
- Running Records – *conduct running records to observe dyslexic learners' reading behaviours, errors, and self-correction rates, gaining insights into their reading strategies and areas for improvement (Clay, 2002).*

Individualised Goal Setting

Collaboratively set individualised reading goals with dyslexic learners to guide their reading development.

Consider the following strategies:

- SMART Goals – *develop Specific, Measurable, Achievable, Relevant, and Time-bound (SMART) goals that align with dyslexic learners' specific reading needs and reflect their desired areas of growth (Locke & Latham, 2002).*
- Incremental Goal Setting – *break down larger reading goals into smaller, achievable milestones, providing dyslexic learners with a sense of progress and accomplishment along their reading journey (Reid et al., 2009).*
- Regular Goal Review – *routinely review and revise reading goals based on dyslexic learners' progress, ensuring that goals remain relevant and challenging yet attainable (Black & William, 2009).*

Assessment Accommodations

When conducting assessments, provide necessary accommodations to ensure dyslexic learners' access to the assessment and a fair representation of their reading abilities.

Consider the following strategies:

- ◎ Extended Time – *allow dyslexic learners additional time to complete assessments, considering their processing speed challenges (Shaywitz et al., 2007).*
- ◎ Alternative Formats – *provide assessments in alternative formats, such as audio recordings or digital versions, to accommodate dyslexic learners' reading difficulties (Blackhurst et al., 2011).*
- ◎ Read-Aloud Support – *offer read-aloud support for assessment instructions or passages to ensure dyslexic learners' comprehension and accurate responses (Rasinski et al., 2005).*

By implementing effective assessment progress monitoring practices, educations can gain valuable insights into dyslexic learners' reading abilities, track their growth, and make informed instructional decisions to support their ongoing development.

Conclusion

The effective implementation of reading and literacy strategies for dyslexic learners is crucial in supporting their reading development and fostering academic success. This chapter has explored various strategies and approaches to address the unique challenges faced by dyslexic learners in reading. By understanding dyslexia and reading difficulties, incorporating phonological awareness and phonics instruction, promoting reading comprehension strategies, facilitating vocabulary development, and utilising assistive technology and accommodations, educators can create a dyslexia-friendly classroom that maximises learning opportunities for dyslexic learners.

Assessment and progress monitoring play a vital role in ensuring targeted support and tracking the progress of dyslexic learners. By conducting diagnostic assessments, implementing progress monitoring techniques, setting individualised goals, and providing assessment accommodations, educators can gain valuable insights into dyslexic learners' reading abilities, tailor instruction to their specific needs, and celebrate their growth along the reading journey.

Creating a dyslexia-friendly classroom also involves cultivating a supportive and inclusive environment. By building rapport, empathy, and understanding, educators can create a safe space where dyslexic learners feel valued and supported. Collaboration with parents, professionals, and specialised support services further strengthens the support network for dyslexic learners.

Differentiated instruction techniques and strategies across content areas help dyslexic learners access and engage with the curriculum, enhancing their overall learning experiences. By recognising the diverse learning needs and styles of dyslexic learners, educators can provide tailored instruction, scaffold learning experiences, and promote self-advocacy and confidence.

In conclusion, by implementing evidence-based reading and literacy strategies, providing appropriate accommodations, fostering a dyslexia-friendly classroom environment, and collaborating with various stakeholders, educators can empower dyslexic learners to overcome reading challenges, develop strong reading skills, and thrive academically. With continued dedication, support, and understanding, dyslexic learners can unlock their full potential and become lifelong readers and learners.

References

Baker, L., & Brown, A. L. (1984). Metacognitive skills and reading. In P. D. Pearson (Ed.), Handbook of reading research (Vol. 1, pp. 353-394). Longman.

Baumann, J. F., et al. (2003). Teaching vocabulary: 50 creative strategies, grades K-12 (2nd ed.). Pearson.

Beck, I. L., et al. (2002). Bringing words to life: Robust vocabulary instruction. Guilford Press.

Black, P., & Wiliam, D. (2009). Developing the theory of formative assessment. Educational Assessment, Evaluation and Accountability, 21(1), 5-31.

Blackhurst, A. E., et al. (2011). Using speech recognition software to enhance writing skills of students with learning disabilities: A literature review. Learning Disabilities: A Contemporary Journal, 9(2), 129-145.

Catts, H. W., & Kamhi, A. G. (2017). Language and reading disabilities. Pearson.

Clay, M. M. (2002). An observation survey of early literacy achievement (3rd ed.). Heinemann.

Dole, J. A., et al. (1991). Learning from informational text: Effects of strategy instruction and reciprocal teaching. Reading Research Quarterly, 26(3), 250-276.

Dweck, C. S. (2006). Mindset: The new psychology of success. Random House.

Duke, N. K., & Pearson, P. D. (2002). Effective practices for developing reading comprehension. In A. E. Farstrup & S. J. Samuels (Eds.), What research has to say about reading instruction (3rd ed., pp. 205-242). International Reading Association.

Ehri, L. C., et al. (2001). Systematic phonics instruction helps students learn to read: Evidence from the National Reading Panel's meta-analysis. Review of Educational Research, 71(3), 393-447.

Ehri, L. C., et al. (2021). Supporting dyslexic readers: An overview of digital reading technology tools. Perspectives on Language and Literacy, 47(1), 31-39.

Fountas, I. C., & Pinnell, G. S. (2017). Guided reading: Responsive teaching across the grades. Heinemann.

Fuchs, L. S., & Fuchs, D. (2006). Introduction to response to intervention: What, why, and how valid is it? Reading Research Quarterly, 41(1), 93-99.

Fuchs, L. S., et al. (2001). Peer-assisted learning strategies: An evidence-based practice to promote reading achievement. Learning Disabilities Research & Practice, 16(4), 203-214.

Gambrell, L. B., & Koskinen, P. S. (2003). Chapter 7: Enhancing comprehension through questioning. In L. B. Gambrell, L. M. Morrow, & M. Pressley (Eds.), Best practices in literacy instruction (2nd ed., pp. 107-126). Guilford Press.

Gentry, J. R., et al. (2013). E-readers and the collaborative classroom: Opportunities and challenges. The Reading Teacher, 67(7), 570-580.

Goodwin, A. P., & Ahn, S. (2010). A meta-analysis of morphological interventions in English: Effects on literacy outcomes for school-age children. Scientific Studies of Reading, 14(3), 301-322.

Graham, S., & Harris, K. R. (2005). Writing better: Effective strategies for teaching students with learning difficulties. Brookes Publishing.

Graves, M. F. (2006). The vocabulary book: Learning and instruction. Teachers College Press.

Hattie, J., & Timperley, H. (2007). The power of feedback. Review of Educational Research, 77(1), 81-112.

Heim, S., et al. (2015). Text-to-speech and related read-aloud tools for improving reading and spelling skills in students with reading disabilities: A systematic review. Campbell Systematic Reviews, 11(5), 1-122.

Higgins, E. L., & Raskind, M. H. (2005). Assistive technology for reading. In H. L. Swanson, K. R. Harris, & S. Graham (Eds.), Handbook of learning disabilities (pp. 423-436). Guilford Press.

Hulme, C., & Snowling, M. J. (2009). Developmental disorders of language learning and cognition. Wiley-Blackwell.

Hutchinson, N. L., et al. (2003). Improving classroom performance of children with attention-deficit/hyperactivity disorder: Clinical implications of recent research findings. Journal of Pediatric Psychology, 28(8), 635-646.

Johns, J. L. (2017). Basic reading inventory: Pre-primer through grade twelve and early literacy assessments (11th ed.). Kendall Hunt.

Kuhn, M. R., et al. (2010). Helping struggling readers with fluency: Collaborative strategic reading and repeated reading. Intervention in School and Clinic, 46(2), 87-97.

Locke, E. A., & Latham, G. P. (2002). Building a practically useful theory of goal setting and task motivation: A 35-year odyssey. American Psychologist, 57(9), 705-717.

Lyon, G. R., et al. (2003). Report of the National Reading Panel. Teaching children to read: An evidence-based assessment of the scientific research literature on reading and its implications for reading instruction. National Institute of Child Health and Human Development.

Marzano, R. J., et al. (2001). Building background knowledge for academic achievement: Research on what works in schools. ASCD.

McKool, S. S., et al. (2010). Developing reading fluency with repeated reading and phrase-cued reading. Intervention in School and Clinic, 45(3), 143-150.

Moats, L. C., & Dakin, K. E. (2008). Basic facts about dyslexia and other reading problems (2nd ed.). Brookes Publishing.

Nagy, W., & Anderson, R. C. (1984). How many words are there in printed school English? Reading Research Quarterly, 19(3), 304-330.

Nagy, W. E., et al. (2005). Morphological awareness, vocabulary, and reading. Reading Research Quarterly, 40(3), 378-385.

Nation, K. (2005). Children's reading difficulties: An overview. In M. J. Snowling & C. Hulme (Eds.), The science of reading: A handbook (pp. 248-266). Blackwell.

National Reading Panel. (2000). Teaching children to read: An evidence-based assessment of the scientific research literature on reading and its implications for reading instruction. National Institute of Child Health and Human Development.

Ogle, D. M. (1986). K-W-L: A teaching model that develops active reading of expository text. The Reading Teacher, 39(6), 564-570.

Orton, S. T. (1937). Reading, writing, and speech problems in children: A presentation of certain types of disorders in the development of the language faculty. W. W. Norton & Company.

Pressley, M., & Afflerbach, P. (1995). Verbal protocols of reading: The nature of constructively responsive reading. Lawrence Erlbaum.

Pumfrey, P. D., & Reason, R. D. (2001). The effects of colored overlays on reading achievement. Journal of Research in Reading, 24(1), 41-56.

Rasinski, T. V. (2011). Why fluency should be hot! The Reading Teacher, 65(8), 516-521.

Rasinski, T. V., et al. (2005). The effects of reading interventions on the fluency and comprehension of fourth-grade students: A randomized trial. Reading Research Quarterly, 40(2), 148-182.

Reid, R., et al. (2009). Strategy instruction for students with learning disabilities (2nd ed.). Guilford Press.

Rosenshine, B., & Meister, C. (1994). Reciprocal teaching: A review of the research. Review of Educational Research, 64(4), 479-530.

Shaywitz, S. E., & Shaywitz, B. A. (2008). Paying attention to reading: The neurobiology of reading and dyslexia. Development and Psychopathology, 20(4), 1329-1349.

Shaywitz, S. E., et al. (2007). Disability profiles of reading-disabled and nondisabled children and adolescents. Journal of Developmental & Behavioral Pediatrics, 28(4), 262-270.

Simmons, D. C., & Kame'enui, E. J. (1998). Curriculum-based assessment in reading: A handbook of practical strategies. Allyn & Bacon.

Snow, C. E., et al. (1998). Preventing reading difficulties in young children. National Academy Press.

Snowling, M. J., & Hulme, C. (2012). Annual research review: The nature and classification of reading disorders - a commentary on proposals for DSM-5. Journal of Child Psychology and Psychiatry, 53(5), 593-607.

Swanson, H. L. (2003). Working memory in learning disabilities: Issues within instruction-oriented research. Journal of Learning Disabilities, 36(6), 556-563.

Therrien, W. J., et al. (2006). The effects of repeated readings and attentional cues on reading fluency and comprehension: A case study. Journal of Behavioral Education, 15(1), 45-63.

Tomlinson, C. A., & Moon, T. R. (2013). Assessment and student success in a differentiated classroom. ASCD.

Torgesen, J. K., et al. (2001). Individual differences in response to early interventions in reading: The lingering problem of treatment resisters. Learning Disabilities Research & Practice, 16(1), 55-64.

Vacca, R. T., et al. (2014). Content area reading: Literacy and learning across the curriculum (11th ed.). Pearson.

Vanderwood, M. L., et al. (2012). Designing digital content to improve reading outcomes for dyslexic students. International Journal of Special Education, 27(1), 16-29.

Vidyasagar, T. R., & Pammer, K. (2010). Dyslexia: A deficit in visuo-spatial attention, not in phonological processing. Trends in Cognitive Sciences, 14(2), 57-63.

CHAPTER FIVE

Written Expression and Spelling Support

Introduction

Written expression and spelling are fundamental aspects of literacy that play a crucial role in academic achievement and communication. For dyslexic learners, however, these areas often present unique challenges. Dyslexia, a specific learning disorder affecting reading and language processing, can significantly impact a student's ability to express themselves effectively in writing and accurately spell words. This chapter explores strategies and support systems aimed at helping dyslexic learners overcome these challenges and develop their skills in written expression and spelling. By understanding the underlying difficulties, implementing evidence-based practices, and providing targeted interventions, educators can empower dyslexic learners to improve their writing abilities and gain confidence in their written communication. Throughout this chapter, we will delve into various aspects of written expression and spelling support, highlighting effective instructional approaches, assistive technology tools, accommodations, and collaborative efforts to create an inclusive and supportive learning environment for dyslexic learners.

Understanding Dyslexia and Written Expression

Understanding the impact of dyslexia on written expression is essential for educators to provide effective support to dyslexic learners in developing their writing skills. This section explores the specific challenges dyslexic learners face in written expression and the underlying factors contributing to these difficulties.

Written Expression Challenges for Dyslexic Learners

Dyslexic learners often encounter various challenges in written expression, including:

◎ Spelling Difficulties – *dyslexia is commonly associated with difficulties in phonological processing, which can affect spelling accuracy and the ability to apply spelling rules effectively (Bruck, 1990).*

◎ Sentence Structure and Organisation – *dyslexic learners may struggle with sentence construction, maintaining coherence, and organising their ideas logically (Berninger & Swanson, 1994).*

◎ Vocabulary Limitations – *difficulties in word retrieval, understanding word meanings, and using appropriate vocabulary may hinder dyslexic learners' written expression (Catts & Kamhi, 2017).*

◎ Grammar and Punctuation Errors – *dyslexic learners may demonstrate challenges in applying grammar and punctuation rules accurately, leading to errors in written work (Dockrell et al., 2007).*

Underlying Factors

Dyslexia is rooted in neurobiological differences that impact language processing and learning. The following factors contribute to the difficulties dyslexic learners face in written expression:

◎ Phonological Processing Deficits – *dyslexic learners often exhibit weaknesses in phonological awareness, making it challenging to segment and manipulate sounds in words, which can affect spelling and writing skills (Snowling, 2000).*

◎ Working Memory Limitations – *difficulties in working memory, which involves holding and manipulating information in the mind, can affect the ability to organise thoughts, plan writing, and apply grammar and punctuation rules (Swanson & Siegel, 2001).*

- ◉ Processing Speed Deficits – *dyslexic learners may experience slower processing speed, impacting the efficiency and fluency of their writing production (Wolf & Bowers, 1999).*
- ◉ Language Processing Difficulties – *dyslexia involves difficulties in processing and understanding language, which can manifest in challenges with vocabulary, grammar, and comprehension, all of which influence written expression (Hulme & Snowling, 2009).*

Understanding the specific challenges dyslexic learners face in written expression and recognising the underlying factors at play can inform instructional practices and interventions that effectively address their needs. By employing evidence-based strategies and providing targeted support, educators can help dyslexic learners overcome barriers and develop their writing skills.

Phonological Awareness and Spelling Instruction

Phonological awareness plays a crucial role in spelling development for dyslexic learners. This section explores the significance of phonological awareness and effective strategies for spelling instruction that promotes phonological skills.

Importance of Phonological Awareness

Phonological awareness refers to the ability to recognise and manipulate the sounds of spoken language. It is a foundational skill for spelling, as dyslexic learners need to understand the sound-symbol correspondence in order to accurately represent words in written form (Ehri, 2014). Phonological awareness allows dyslexic learners to break word into individual sounds (phonemes), identify patterns, and manipulate sounds to form words (Gillon, 2018).

Explicit Phonological Instruction

Explicit instruction in phonological awareness can significantly improve spelling skills for dyslexic learners.

Key strategies include:

- ◉ Phonemic Awareness Activities – *engage dyslexic learners in various activities that focus on identifying, segmenting, blending, and manipulating individual sounds within word (Ehri et al., 2001).*

◎ Sounds-Symbol Correspondence – *teach dyslexic learners the relationship between sounds and letters, emphasising phoneme-grapheme mapping and teaching spelling patterns (Moats & Dakin, 2008).*

◎ Multi-sensory Approaches – *incorporate multi-sensory techniques, such as using manipulative, visual aids, and kinaesthetic movements, to reinforce phonological concepts (Orton-Gillingham, 1935).*

Spelling Strategies

Dyslexic learners benefit from specific spelling strategies that emphasise phonological awareness.

Consider the following approaches:

◎ Sound Mapping – *encourage dyslexic learners to map out the sounds in words using symbols or boxes to represent each phoneme (Simmons & Kame'enui, 1998).*

◎ Word Families and Analogies – *teach dyslexic learners to identify common word patterns and use analogies to apply spelling rules and patterns across related words (Bear et al., 2008).*

◎ Morphological Analysis – *explore word structure and teach dyslexic learners to identify meaningful word parts (prefixes, suffixes, roots) that can assist in spelling and decoding (Carlisle, 2000).*

Word Study and Vocabulary Development

Integrating word study activities and vocabulary development supports dyslexic learners' spelling skills.

Consider these strategies:

◎ Word Sorter – *engage dyslexic learners in word sorting activities where they categorise words based on spelling patterns, phonetic features, or word families (Bear et al., 2008).*

◎ Contextual Spelling Practice – *encourage dyslexic learners to apply spelling skills in meaningful contexts, such as writing sentences or short passages (Ganske, 2000).*

◎ Vocabulary Instruction – *provide explicit vocabulary instruction, including teaching the spelling, meaning, and usage of words, to encourage both spelling and word knowledge (Beck et al., 2013).*

By incorporating explicit phonological awareness instruction, implementing effective spelling strategies, and integrating word study and vocabulary development, educators can support dyslexic learners in developing their spelling skills and improving their overall written expression.

Vocabulary Development and Word Choice

Developing a rich vocabulary and using appropriate word choice are essential components of effective written expression for dyslexic learners. This section explores strategies and approaches to support vocabulary development and enhance word choice skills in dyslexic learners.

Importance of Vocabulary Development

Vocabulary knowledge is a key factor in improving reading comprehension, written expression, and overall communication skills. Dyslexic learners may face challenges in acquiring and using vocabulary effectively due to their difficulties in word retrieval and word meaning (Catts & Kamhi, 2017). Therefore, explicit vocabulary instruction is crucial to support their written expression.

Explicit Vocabulary Instruction

Dyslexic learners benefit from explicit instruction that focuses on building their vocabulary knowledge. Consider the following strategies:

- ◎ Contextual Vocabulary Instruction - *Teach vocabulary words in meaningful contexts, providing opportunities for dyslexic learners to encounter and use new words in authentic reading and writing activities (Beck et al., 2013).*
- ◎ Word Maps or Concept Cards - *Help dyslexic learners organize and connect new vocabulary words by creating word maps or concept cards that include word definitions, synonyms, antonyms, and example sentences (Marzano, 2004).*
- ◎ Word Learning Strategies - *Teach dyslexic learners' specific strategies for learning and retaining new vocabulary, such as using*

mnemonic devices, creating associations, or using visual imagery (Nation, 2009).

Word Choice and Expression

Supporting dyslexic learners in using appropriate word choice enhances their written expression. Consider the following strategies:

- ◎ Synonym and Antonym Activities - *Engage dyslexic learners in activities that explore synonyms and antonyms to expand their vocabulary and provide alternatives for word choice (Graves, 2016).*
- ◎ Precision in Language - *Encourage dyslexic learners to choose precise words that convey their intended meaning, emphasising the importance of using specific nouns, vivid adjectives, and strong verbs (Harris, 2008).*
- ◎ Editing for Word Choice - *Teach dyslexic learners to review and revise their written work with a focus on word choice, helping them refine their expression and select the most appropriate words for their intended message (Graham & Perin, 2007).*

Contextual Reading and Writing Experiences

Providing dyslexic learners with rich reading and writing experiences in various contexts supports their vocabulary development and word choice skills. Consider these approaches:

- ◎ Wide Reading - *Encourage dyslexic learners to read a variety of texts, including fiction, nonfiction, and informational materials, to encounter new words and expand their vocabulary (Nagy & Herman, 1987).*
- ◎ Writing Across Genres - *Engage dyslexic learners in diverse writing tasks across different genres, allowing them to practice using vocabulary in different contexts and for different purposes (Graham et al., 2012).*
- ◎ Word-Rich Environments - *Create a word-rich classroom environment that exposes dyslexic learners to words through word walls, anchor charts, and displays, fostering vocabulary growth through visual supports (Bear et al., 2008).*

By incorporating explicit vocabulary instruction, promoting word choice strategies, and providing ample opportunities for contextual reading and writing experiences, educators can support dyslexic learners in expanding their vocabulary repertoire and using words effectively in their written expression.

Sentence and Paragraph Structure

Developing effective sentence and paragraph structure is essential for dyslexic learners to express their ideas clearly and coherently in written form. This section explores strategies and approaches to support dyslexic learners in improving their sentence and paragraph structure skills.

Understanding Sentence Structure

Dyslexic learners may struggle with sentence structure, including sentence construction, sentence variety, and maintaining coherence. The following strategies can help address these challenges:

- ◎ Explicit Instruction - *Provide explicit instruction on sentence components (subject, verb, object), sentence types (declarative, interrogative, imperative), and sentence combining techniques (using coordinating conjunctions, subordinating clauses) (Berninger & Richards, 2017).*
- ◎ Modelling and Guided Practice - *Model and guide dyslexic learners through the process of constructing well-formed sentences, emphasizing proper punctuation and sentence organization (Graham & Perin, 2007).*
- ◎ Sentence Frames and Starters - *Offer sentence frames and starters to support dyslexic learners in structuring their sentences, providing scaffolding and promoting sentence variety (Strong et al., 2004).*

Developing Paragraph Structure

Dyslexic learners often encounter challenges in organising their ideas into coherent paragraphs. Consider the following strategies to support their paragraph development skills:

- ◎ Graphic Organisers - *Use graphic organisers, such as webs, outlines, or story maps, to help dyslexic learners visually organise their ideas before writing paragraphs (Hochman & Wexler, 2017).*
- ◎ Topic and Concluding Sentences - *Teach dyslexic learners the importance of topic sentences to introduce paragraph content and concluding sentences to summarise key points (Bear et al., 2008).*

⊚ Transitions and Cohesion - *Emphasise the use of transitional words and phrases (e.g., first, next, therefore) to create cohesive paragraphs that flow smoothly (Graham et al., 2012).*

Cohesion and Coherence

Dyslexic learners may struggle with maintaining cohesion and coherence within and between sentences and paragraphs. Consider the following strategies to enhance their writing cohesion:

⊚ Sentence-Level Cohesion - *Teach dyslexic learners to use pronouns, conjunctions, and transitional words to connect ideas within sentences and create smooth transitions (Graham et al., 2012).*

⊚ Paragraph-Level Cohesion - *Help dyslexic learners develop skills in organising and linking ideas across paragraphs, using cohesive devices such as repetition of key words or phrases and explicit references (Berninger & Richards, 2017).*

⊚ Editing and Revising - *Guide dyslexic learners in reviewing their writing for clarity, ensuring that sentences and paragraphs are logically connected and ideas flow coherently (Graham & Perin, 2007).*

By providing explicit instruction on sentence structure, supporting paragraph development, and fostering cohesion and coherence, educators can empower dyslexic learners to express their thoughts and ideas effectively through well-structured sentences and paragraphs.

Grammar and Punctuation Support

Developing proficiency in grammar and punctuation is crucial for dyslexic learners to convey their ideas accurately and effectively in written form. This section explores strategies and approaches to provide support for dyslexic learners in improving their grammar and punctuation skills.

Explicit Grammar Instruction

Dyslexic learners can benefit from explicit instruction that focuses on teaching grammar rules and conventions. Consider the following strategies:

- ◎ Direct Teaching - *Provide explicit explanations of grammar concepts and rules, breaking them down into manageable components, and providing ample examples (Harris, 2008).*
- ◎ Scaffolded Practice - *Offer guided practice activities that gradually increase in complexity, allowing dyslexic learners to apply grammar rules in context (Graham et al., 2012).*
- ◎ Error Analysis - *Engage dyslexic learners in error analysis tasks, where they identify and correct grammar errors in sample sentences, helping them develop error awareness and self-editing skills (Beers, 2003).*

Visual Supports and Graphic Organisers

Dyslexic learners often benefit from visual supports and graphic organisers to reinforce grammar concepts and aid in understanding. Consider the following strategies:

- ◎ Anchor Charts and Posters - *Create visual aids, such as anchor charts or posters, that display grammar rules, sentence structures, and punctuation guidelines for dyslexic learners to refer to during writing tasks (Bear et al., 2008).*
- ◎ Sentence Frames - *Provide sentence frames or templates that incorporate correct grammar structures, helping dyslexic learners practice using grammatically accurate sentences (Strong et al., 2004).*
- ◎ Graphic Organisers - *Use graphic organisers, such as flowcharts or diagrams, to visually represent grammar concepts, sentence structures, and punctuation rules (Hochman & Wexler, 2017).*

Editing and Proofreading Strategies

Teaching dyslexic learners effective editing and proofreading strategies can enhance their grammar and punctuation skills. Consider the following strategies:

- ◎ Editing Checklists - *Provide dyslexic learners with checklists that outline common grammar and punctuation errors to look for during the editing process (Graham & Perin, 2007).*
- ◎ Peer Editing - *Encourage dyslexic learners to engage in peer editing activities, where they exchange written work with peers and provide*

feedback on grammar and punctuation usage (Graham et al., 2012).

◎ Technology Tools - *Introduce dyslexic learners to grammar and spell-checking software or online tools that can assist in identifying and correcting grammar and punctuation errors (Nation, 2009).*

Grammar and Punctuation in Context

It is essential to emphasise the application of grammar and punctuation skills in meaningful writing contexts. Consider the following strategies:

◎ Authentic Writing Tasks - *Engage dyslexic learners in writing activities that require them to apply grammar and punctuation rules in authentic contexts, such as writing narratives, reports, or persuasive essays (Graham et al., 2012).*

◎ Mentor Texts - *Expose dyslexic learners to well-written texts, using them as models to analyse and identify effective grammar and punctuation usage (Harris, 2008).*

◎ Sentence Combining - *Provide opportunities for dyslexic learners to practice combining simple sentences into more complex and compound sentences, reinforcing grammar and punctuation rules (Strong et al., 2004).*

By providing explicit grammar instruction, incorporating visual supports and graphic organisers, teaching effective editing and proofreading strategies, and emphasising grammar and punctuation skills in authentic writing contexts, educators can support dyslexic learners in developing their grammar and punctuation proficiency.

Planning and Editing Strategies

Planning and editing are essential components of the writing process for dyslexic learners, supporting them in producing well-structured and coherent written work. This section explores strategies and approaches to assist dyslexic learners in planning and editing their writing effectively.

Pre-Writing Strategies

Dyslexic learners can benefit from pre-writing strategies that help them organise their thoughts and plan their writing. Consider the following approaches:

- ◎ Mind Mapping or Brainstorming - *Encourage dyslexic learners to create visual diagrams or lists to generate ideas and organise their thoughts before starting the writing process (Fawcett & Nicolson, 2018).*
- ◎ Story boarding - *Use storyboards or graphic organisers to help dyslexic learners plan narratives or essays, providing a visual framework for organising ideas and sequencing events (Ofsted, 2011).*
- ◎ Planning templates - *Provide dyslexic learners with planning templates that guide them through the process of outlining their writing, including sections such as introduction, main points, and conclusion (Department for Education, 2012).*

Editing Strategies

Dyslexic learners benefit from explicit instruction and strategies for editing their writing. Consider the following approaches:

- ◎ Read-Aloud and Self-Reading - *Encourage dyslexic learners to read their written work aloud, as it can help them identify errors, awkward phrasing, and missing punctuation (Berninger & Richards, 2017).*
- ◎ Peer or Teacher Feedback - *Facilitate peer or teacher feedback sessions where dyslexic learners receive constructive feedback on their writing, including suggestions for improving grammar, punctuation, and clarity (Ofsted, 2011).*
- ◎ Editing Checklists - *Provide dyslexic learners with checklists that outline common grammar, punctuation, and spelling errors to look for during the editing process (Fawcett & Nicolson, 2018).*

Spelling Support

Dyslexic learners often encounter challenges in spelling. Consider the following strategies to support spelling in the planning and editing stages:

- ◎ Word Banks - *Provide dyslexic learners with word banks related to the writing topic, offering alternative spelling options or commonly misspelled words for reference (Department for Education, 2012).*
- ◎ Spelling Aids - *Introduce dyslexic learners to spelling aids, such as*

electronic dictionaries or spell-checking software, to assist in identifying and correcting spelling errors (Reid, 2016).

◎ Mnemonic Devices - *Teach dyslexic learners' mnemonic devices or memory strategies to help them remember spelling patterns, irregular words, or specific spelling rules (British Dyslexia Association, 2018).*

By incorporating pre-writing strategies, teaching effective editing techniques, and providing spelling support, educators can empower dyslexic learners to plan their writing effectively and edit their work for clarity, accuracy, and coherence.

Assistive Technology and Writing Tools

Assistive technology and writing tools can significantly support dyslexic learners in overcoming writing challenges and enhancing their written expression. This section explores various assistive technology options and writing tools that can empower dyslexic learners in the writing process.

Text-to-Speech Software

Text-to-speech software, such as speech synthesis or screen reading tools, can assist dyslexic learners in the writing process. Consider the following benefits:

◎ Reading Support - *Dyslexic learners can listen to their written work being read aloud, helping them identify errors, improve sentence structure, and enhance overall coherence (Reid, 2016).*

◎ Editing Assistance - *By hearing their words read back to them, dyslexic learners can detect grammar and punctuation errors, as well as awkward phrasing or incomplete sentences (British Dyslexia Association, 2018).*

◎ Multi-sensory Approach - *Text-to-speech tools provide a multi-sensory experience, allowing dyslexic learners to hear and see the text simultaneously, reinforcing reading and writing connections (Hitchcock et al., 2018).*

Speech-to-Text Software

Speech-to-text software, also known as voice recognition or dictation software, can be valuable for dyslexic learners who struggle with writing mechanics. Consider the following advantages:

- ◎ Enhanced Productivity - *Dyslexic learners can dictate their thoughts and ideas, bypassing handwriting or typing difficulties, and producing written work more efficiently (Reid, 2016).*
- ◎ Reduced Spelling and Typing Challenges - *Speech-to-text software automatically converts spoken words into written text, minimising concerns about spelling errors or keyboarding skills (British Dyslexia Association, 2018).*
- ◎ Focus on Content Generation - *By removing the physical demands of writing, dyslexic learners can concentrate on expressing their ideas without being hindered by spelling or motor challenges (Reid, 2016).*

Word Prediction and Spelling Support

Word prediction and spelling support tools can aid dyslexic learners in improving spelling accuracy and word choice. Consider the following features:

- ◎ Word Suggestions - *These tools provide word suggestions based on the context of what dyslexic learners are writing, assisting in word retrieval, and reducing spelling errors (Hitchcock et al., 2018).*
- ◎ Phonemic Support - *Some tools offer phonetic spelling options, helping dyslexic learners choose the correct spelling for words they struggle with (British Dyslexia Association, 2018).*
- ◎ Customisation - *Dyslexic learners can often personalise word prediction settings to accommodate their specific spelling patterns and vocabulary needs (Reid, 2016).*

Graphic Organisers and Writing Support Software

Graphic organisers and writing support software can assist dyslexic learners in organising their ideas and improving overall writing structure. Consider the following benefits:

- ◎ Visual Organisation - *Graphic organisers provide dyslexic learners with visual frameworks for planning and structuring their writing, facilitating coherence and logical flow (Fawcett & Nicolson, 2018).*
- ◎ Sentence and Paragraph Guides - *Writing support software may*

include built-in sentence starters, paragraph templates, or structural guides to support dyslexic learners in constructing well-formed sentences and paragraphs (Reid, 2016).

◉ Grammar and Spell-Checking - *Many writing support tools incorporate grammar and spell-checking features, assisting dyslexic learners in identifying and correcting errors (British Dyslexia Association, 2018).*

By integrating assistive technology tools such as text-to-speech software, speech-to-text software, word prediction and spelling support tools, and graphic organisers, educators can empower dyslexic learners with the necessary writing tools to overcome challenges and enhance their writing abilities.

Accommodations for Written Expression and Spelling

Implementing appropriate accommodations can greatly support dyslexic learners in overcoming challenges related to written expression and spelling. This section explores a range of accommodations that can be implemented to create an inclusive learning environment for dyslexic learners.

Extended Time for Writing Assignments

Providing dyslexic learners with extended time for writing assignments allows them to work at their own pace, alleviating time pressure and enabling them to focus on producing high-quality written work (National Center for Learning Disabilities, n.d.). This accommodation recognises the processing difficulties dyslexic learners may experience and allows them to demonstrate their full potential.

Use of Assistive Technology

Leveraging assistive technology tools can significantly enhance dyslexic learners' written expression and spelling skills. Consider the following accommodations:

◉ Text-to-Speech Software - *Allowing dyslexic learners to use text-to-speech software enables them to listen to their written work,* aiding in identifying errors, improving sentence structure, and enhancing overall coherence (Reid, 2016).

- ◎ Speech-to-Text Software - *Permitting dyslexic learners to use speech-to-text software supports them in overcoming spelling challenges and focusing on content generation rather than the mechanics of writing (British Dyslexia Association, 2018).*
- ◎ Word Prediction Tools - *Enabling dyslexic learners to use word prediction software helps them with spelling accuracy and word choice, providing suggestions based on context and reducing spelling errors (Hitchcock et al., 2018).*

Access to Spelling Resources
Providing dyslexic learners with access to spelling resources can support their spelling accuracy and confidence. Consider the following accommodations:

- ◎ Personalised Word Banks - *Allowing dyslexic learners to create and maintain personalised word banks or dictionaries with commonly used words and words they frequently struggle with (Reid, 2016).*
- ◎ Spelling References - *Providing dyslexic learners with spelling references, such as word lists, dictionaries, or online resources, assists them in independently verifying spelling and building their spelling repertoire (Fawcett & Nicolson, 2018).*

Alternative Modes of Expression
Offering dyslexic learners' alternative modes of expression acknowledges their strengths and provides opportunities for creativity and engagement. Consider the following accommodations:

- ◎ Oral Presentations - *Allowing dyslexic learners to present their ideas orally instead of relying solely on written assignments enables them to showcase their knowledge and communication skills (National Center for Learning Disabilities, n.d.).*
- ◎ Visual Representations - *Permitting dyslexic learners to use visual aids, such as diagrams, charts, or drawings, to convey their understanding or demonstrate concepts provides an alternative means of expressing themselves (Fawcett & Nicolson, 2018).*

Grammar and Spell-Checking Assistance

Assisting dyslexic learners with grammar and spell-checking can support their writing accuracy. Consider the following accommodations:

- ◉ Grammar and Spell-Checking Tools - *Encouraging dyslexic learners to use grammar and spell-checking features available in word processing software or online tools helps them identify and correct errors (British Dyslexia Association, 2018).*
- ◉ Peer or Teacher Proofreading - *Offering dyslexic learners opportunities for peer or teacher proofreading provides them with additional support in identifying and correcting grammar and spelling errors (Reid, 2016).*

By implementing appropriate accommodations such as extended time, assistive technology tools, access to spelling resources, alternative modes of expression, and grammar and spell-checking assistance, educators can create an inclusive learning environment that supports dyslexic learners' written expression and spelling development.

Building Confidence and Self-Efficacy

Building confidence and self-efficacy in dyslexic learners is essential for fostering a positive mindset and empowering them to succeed in written expression and spelling. This section explores strategies and approaches to support the development of confidence and self-efficacy in dyslexic learners.

Emphasise Strengths and Progress

Acknowledge and celebrate the strengths and progress of dyslexic learners in their written expression and spelling skills. Highlight their accomplishments, improvements, and unique talents to boost their confidence and self-belief (Fawcett & Nicolson, 2018). Recognise that dyslexic learners have valuable perspectives and strengths that can contribute to their writing.

Provide Constructive Feedback

Offer constructive feedback that focuses on specific areas of improvement while highlighting the positive aspects of dyslexic learners' written work. Provide clear guidance on how they can enhance their writing skills and offer strategies for addressing challenges (Reid, 2016). Encouragement and targeted feedback help dyslexic learners see their potential and believe in their ability to improve.

Encourage Self-Reflection and Self-Advocacy

Foster self-reflection and self-advocacy skills in dyslexic learners. Encourage them to reflect on their writing strengths and areas for growth, identify strategies that work best for them, and express their needs to teachers and peers (Hitchcock et al., 2018). Developing self-awareness and advocating for their learning preferences can empower dyslexic learners to take ownership of their writing journey.

Promote a Growth Mindset

Cultivate a growth mindset in dyslexic learners by emphasising that abilities can be developed through effort, practice, and effective strategies (Dweck, 2006). Encourage them to view challenges as opportunities for growth and embrace mistakes as learning experiences. Help dyslexic learners recognise that progress in writing is achievable and that their effort and perseverance are valued.

Provide a Supportive Learning Environment

Foster a supportive learning environment that values and respects the unique strengths and challenges of dyslexic learners. Create a classroom culture that promotes inclusivity, where mistakes are seen as opportunities for learning, and all students feel comfortable taking risks in their writing (Fawcett & Nicolson, 2018). Encourage collaboration and peer support, allowing dyslexic learners to share their experiences and learn from their peers.

Set Realistic and Attainable Goals

Help dyslexic learners set realistic and attainable goals in their writing. Break down larger writing tasks into smaller, manageable steps, allowing them to experience success and build confidence incrementally. Adjust expectations and provide appropriate scaffolding to ensure that dyslexic learners can meet their goals and experience a sense of accomplishment (Reid, 2016).

By emphasising strengths, providing constructive feedback, fostering self-reflection and self-advocacy, promoting a growth mindset, creating a supportive learning environment, and setting realistic goals, educators can nurture the confidence and self-efficacy of dyslexic learners in their written expression and spelling abilities.

Collaboration with Parents and Professionals

Collaborating with parents and professionals is crucial in supporting dyslexic learners' written expression and spelling development. This section explores effective strategies and approaches to foster collaboration and create a unified support system for dyslexic learners.

Open and Regular Communication

Establish open and regular communication channels with parents and professionals involved in supporting dyslexic learners. Maintain ongoing dialogue to exchange information, share insights, and discuss progress, challenges, and strategies (Fawcett & Nicolson, 2018). Regular communication helps ensure that all stakeholders are well-informed and aligned in supporting the learner's needs.

Share Assessment and Progress Information

Share assessment findings, progress reports, and any relevant information with parents and professionals involved in the learner's support team. Provide clear explanations of assessment results, highlight strengths and areas for improvement, and discuss implications for written expression and spelling (Reid, 2016). Collaboratively identify strategies and interventions that can be implemented across different settings.

Parent Education and Support

Offer parent education sessions or resources focused on dyslexia, written expression, and spelling support strategies. Provide information on effective accommodations, assistive technology tools, and strategies that parents can implement at home to reinforce learning (British Dyslexia Association, 2018). Empower parents with knowledge and resources to actively support their child's writing development.

Individualised Education Plans

Collaborate with parents and professionals to develop individualised support plans that address the specific writing needs of dyslexic learners. Discuss and outline strategies, accommodations, and interventions to be implemented in different contexts, such as home and school (Fawcett & Nicolson, 2018). Ensure that all stakeholders have a shared understanding of the learner's goals and the support required to achieve them.

Regular Progress Monitoring

Establish a system for regular progress monitoring and feedback exchange among parents, professionals, and dyslexic learners. Discuss the learner's progress, identify areas of growth, and collaboratively adjust strategies or interventions as needed (Reid, 2016). Ongoing monitoring helps ensure that support remains tailored to the learner's evolving needs.

Professional Collaboration

Foster collaboration among professionals involved in supporting dyslexic learners, such as teachers, special education specialists, and therapists. Share expertise, collaborate on intervention planning, and coordinate efforts to provide consistent and coherent support across different learning environments (British Dyslexia Association, 2018). Regular meetings or professional development sessions can facilitate this collaboration.

Empathy and Active Listening

Demonstrate empathy and active listening when engaging with parents and professionals. Recognise and respect their perspectives, experiences, and concerns. Create a supportive environment where all stakeholders feel comfortable expressing their thoughts and ideas, contributing to a shared decision-making process (Fawcett & Nicolson, 2018).

By fostering open communication, sharing assessment information, providing parent education and support, developing individualised support plans, implementing regular progress monitoring, promoting professional collaboration, and demonstrating empathy, educators can establish effective collaboration with parents and professionals to support dyslexic learners' written expression and spelling skills.

Conclusions

Supporting dyslexic learners in their written expression and spelling development requires a comprehensive and collaborative approach. Throughout this chapter, we have explored various strategies and considerations to create a supportive learning environment and address the unique challenges faced by dyslexic learners.

By understanding dyslexia and its impact on written expression, educators can tailor their instruction and interventions to meet the specific needs of dyslexic learners. Phonological awareness, spelling instruction, vocabulary development, sentence structure, and grammar support all play vital roles in enhancing written expression skills. Assistive technology tools, accommodations, and differentiated instruction techniques further empower dyslexic learners to overcome barriers and achieve success.

It is crucial to build confidence and self-efficacy in dyslexic learners, celebrating their strengths and progress, and fostering a growth mindset. Collaboration with parents and professionals creates a united support system, ensuring consistency and coherence in the strategies implemented across different settings. Regular communication, sharing of assessment information, and ongoing progress monitoring facilitate a holistic approach to support.

As educators, we can make a profound impact on the written expression and spelling abilities of dyslexic learners. By implementing evidence-based strategies, providing targeted support, and fostering a supportive and inclusive learning environment, we can empower dyslexic learners to reach their full potential and excel in their writing journey.

Remember, each dyslexic learner is unique, and strategies should be adapted to their individual needs. By embracing their strengths, addressing their challenges, and working collaboratively, we can help dyslexic learners thrive in their written expression and spelling skills, enabling them to share their ideas, thoughts, and stories with confidence and clarity.

Together, let us create an inclusive and supportive learning environment that celebrates the diverse talents and abilities of dyslexic learners, recognising that they possess unique perspectives and contributions to the world of written expression.

References

Bear, D. R., et al. (2008). Words their way: Word study for phonics, vocabulary, and spelling instruction (4th ed.). Pearson.

Beck, I. L., et al. (2013). Bringing words to life: Robust vocabulary instruction. Guilford Press.

Beers, K. (2003). When kids can't read: What teachers can do: A guide for teachers, 6-12. Heinemann.

Berninger, V. W., & Richards, T. L. (2017). Brain literacy for educators and psychologists. Academic Press.

Berninger, V. W., & Swanson, H. L. (1994). Modifying Hayes and Flower's model of skilled writing to explain beginning and developing writing. In E. C. Butterfield (Ed.), Children's writing: Toward a process theory of the development of skilled writing (pp. 57-81). JAI Press.

British Dyslexia Association. (2018). Dyslexia-SpLD Trust: Dyslexia style guide. Retrieved from https://dyslex.io/

Bruck, M. (1990). Word-recognition skills of adults with childhood diagnoses of dyslexia. Developmental Psychology, 26(3), 439-454.

Carlisle, J. F. (2000). Awareness of the structure and meaning of morphologically complex words: Impact on reading. Reading and Writing, 12(3-4), 169-190.

Catts, H. W., & Kamhi, A. G. (2017). Language and reading disabilities. Pearson.

Department for Education. (2012). National curriculum in England: English programmes of study. Retrieved from https://www.gov.uk/government/publications/national-curriculum-in-england-english-programmes-of-study

Dockrell, J. E., et al. (2007). Written language outcomes of children with early language delays and difficulties. In R. Paul (Ed.), Language disorders from infancy through adolescence: Assessment and intervention (pp. 233-251). Mosby.

Dweck, C. S. (2006). Mindset: The new psychology of success. Random House.

Ehri, L. C. (2014). Orthographic mapping in the acquisition of sight word reading, spelling memory, and vocabulary learning. Scientific Studies of Reading, 18(1), 5-21.

Ehri, L. C., et al. (2001). Systematic phonics instruction helps students learn to read: Evidence from the National Reading Panel's meta-analysis. Review of Educational Research, 71(3), 393-447.

Fawcett, A. J., & Nicolson, R. I. (2018). Dyslexia: Support in the classroom. Routledge.

Ganske, K. (2000). Word journeys: Assessment-guided phonics, spelling, and vocabulary instruction. The Guilford Press.

Gillon, G. T. (2018). Phonological awareness: From research to practice. Guilford Press.

Graham, S., & Perin, D. (2007). Writing next: Effective strategies to improve writing of adolescents in middle and high schools. Carnegie Corporation of New York.

Graham, S., et al. (2012). Teaching secondary students to write effectively. Carnegie Corporation of New York.

Graves, M. F. (2016). The vocabulary book: Learning and instruction (2nd ed.). Teachers College Press.

Harris, K. R. (2008). Powerful writing strategies for all students. Brookes Publishing.

Hitchcock, C., et al. (2018). Assistive technology for children and young people with specific learning difficulties. Journal of Research in Special Educational Needs, 18(1), 3-14.

Hochman, J., & Wexler, N. (2017). The writing revolution: A guide to advancing thinking through writing in all subjects and grades. Jossey-Bass.

Hulme, C., & Snowling, M. J. (2009). Developmental disorders of language learning and cognition. Wiley-Blackwell.

Marzano, R. J. (2004). Building background knowledge for

academic achievement: Research on what works in schools. ASCD.

Moats, L. C., & Dakin, K. E. (2008). Basic facts about dyslexia and other reading problems (2nd ed.). Brookes Publishing.

Nagy, W., & Herman, P. A. (1987). Breadth and depth of vocabulary knowledge: Implications for acquisition and instruction. In M. G. McKeown & M. E. Curtis (Eds.), The nature of vocabulary acquisition (pp. 19-35). Lawrence Erlbaum Associates.

Nation, K. (2009). Learning vocabulary in another language. Cambridge University Press.

National Center for Learning Disabilities. (n.d.). Accommodations for students with learning disabilities. Retrieved from https://www.understood.org/en/school-learning/partnering-with-child s-school/instructional-strategies/accommodations-for-students-with-le arning-disabilities

Ofsted. (2011). Moving English forward: Action to raise standards in English. Retrieved from https://dera.ioe.ac.uk/20718/

Orton-Gillingham, A. G. (1935). Remedial training for children with specific disability in reading, spelling, and penmanship. Journal of Learning Disabilities, 18(2), 69-82.

Reid, G. (2016). Dyslexia: A complete guide for parents and those who help them (2nd ed.). John Wiley & Sons.

Simmons, D. C., & Kame'enui, E. J. (1998). Curriculum-based measurement in reading: The benchmark assessment system. Pro-Ed.

Snowling, M. J. (2000). Dyslexia (2nd ed.). Blackwell.

Strong, W., et al. (2004). Teaching real-life writing to young learners: Easy teacher-tested lessons that help children learn to write lists, letters, invitations, how-tos, and much more. Scholastic Professional Books.

Swanson, H. L., & Siegel, L. S. (2001). Learning disabilities as a working memory deficit. Issues in Education, 7(1), 1-48.

Wolf, M., & Bowers, P. G. (1999). The double-deficit hypothesis for the developmental dyslexias. Journal of Educational Psychology, 91(3), 415-438.

CHAPTER SIX
Mathematics and Numeracy Support

Introduction

Mathematics is a fundamental subject that plays a significant role in various aspects of our lives. However, for learners with dyslexia, the journey of understanding and excelling in mathematics can present unique challenges. Dyslexia, a specific learning difficulty primarily associated with reading and language processing, can also impact numeracy development, making it essential to address the specific needs of dyslexic learners in this domain.

The aim of this chapter is to explore strategies and approaches for supporting learners with dyslexia in mathematics and numeracy. We will delve into the impact of dyslexia on mathematical learning, considering the cognitive processes involved and the challenges dyslexic learners may face. By understanding the nature of dyslexia in the context of mathematics, educators can tailor their instruction and interventions to meet the specific needs of these learners, empowering them to overcome barriers and develop essential mathematical skills.

Throughout this chapter, we will address various aspects of mathematics support, covering foundational skills, problem-solving strategies, mathematical language and vocabulary development, visual-spatial skills, mathematical anxiety, assistive technology, differentiation, and collaboration with parents and professionals. By exploring evidence-based practices, innovative approaches, and effective instructional techniques, educators can create an inclusive and supportive learning environment that fosters mathematical growth for learners with dyslexia.

It is important to recognise that dyslexic learners possess unique strengths and talents that can be harnessed in their mathematical journey. By embracing a strengths-based approach, leveraging multi-sensory and interactive methods, and providing differentiated instruction, educators can empower dyslexic learners to build mathematical competence, confidence, and enjoyment.

Collaboration among parents, educators, and professionals is also vital in supporting dyslexic learners in mathematics. By working together, sharing insights, and maintaining open lines of communication, we can create a cohesive support system that maximises the potential of these learners.

Ultimately, our goal is to equip educators with the knowledge, strategies, and resources necessary to provide effective mathematics and numeracy support for learners with dyslexia. Through targeted interventions, empathetic instruction, and a commitment to individualised learning, we can help dyslexic learners thrive in the world of mathematics and develop the critical skills needed for their academic and everyday lives.

Together, let us embark on this journey to create an inclusive and empowering mathematical learning experience for learners with dyslexia.

Understanding Dyslexia in the Context of Mathematics

Dyslexia, a specific learning difficulty primarily associated with reading and language processing, can also impact numeracy development and mathematical understanding. In this section, we will explore the nature of dyslexia in the context of mathematics, highlighting the challenges dyslexic learners may face and the implications for their mathematical learning.

Dyslexic learners may encounter difficulties in mathematical tasks that require reading, comprehending, and interpreting written instructions, word problems, or mathematical symbols (Fawcett & Nicolson, 2018). They may struggle with recognising and understanding mathematical vocabulary, as well as processing and retaining mathematical information. These challenges can affect their ability to comprehend mathematical concepts and apply them effectively.

One key area of difficulty for dyslexic learners in mathematics is the processing of mathematical symbols and notation. Dyslexia may impact their ability to accurately recognise and differentiate symbols such as +, -, ×, ÷, fractions, decimals, and mathematical signs. Consequently, dyslexic learners may experience challenges in performing calculations, understanding equations, or interpreting mathematical expressions (Reid, 2016).

Dyslexic learners may also struggle with visual-spatial skills, which are crucial for understanding geometric concepts and spatial relationships in mathematics. Difficulties with visual-spatial processing can affect their ability to visualise and manipulate objects mentally, comprehend spatial arrangements, or perceive patterns and symmetry (British Dyslexia Association, 2018).

Working memory, another cognitive process often affected by dyslexia, plays a significant role in mathematical problem-solving. Dyslexic learners may encounter challenges in holding and manipulating information in their working memory, which can hinder their ability to follow multi-step procedures, retain intermediate results, or remember previously learned concepts (Fawcett & Nicolson, 2018).

It is important to note that dyslexia does not necessarily imply a mathematical learning disability known as dyscalculia. While there may be overlapping characteristics, dyslexia primarily affects reading and language, whereas dyscalculia primarily affects mathematical understanding and numerical operations (Reid, 2016). However, dyslexic learners can still experience specific challenges in mathematical learning that require targeted support and interventions.

Understanding the specific challenges dyslexic learners face in mathematics is essential for educators. By recognising the impact of dyslexia on numeracy development and the cognitive processes involved in mathematical thinking, educators can design instructional strategies and interventions that address the unique needs of dyslexic learners. Implementing multi-sensory approaches, providing visual aids, incorporating explicit instruction, and focusing on building foundational skills can help dyslexic learners overcome barriers and develop mathematical competence.

By adopting a supportive and inclusive approach to mathematics education, educators can empower dyslexic learners to build mathematical confidence, enhance their problem-solving abilities, and experience success in the world of mathematics.

Building Mathematical Foundations

Building strong mathematical foundations is crucial for supporting dyslexic learners in developing numeracy skills and mathematical understanding. In this section, we will explore strategies and activities aimed at strengthening the fundamental building blocks of mathematics.

Number Sense and Counting

Develop dyslexic learners' number sense by providing opportunities for hands-on exploration, manipulatives, and real-life contexts. Engage learners in activities that promote counting, subitising (instantly recognising the number of objects without counting) and understanding the magnitude and relationships between numbers (Fawcett & Nicolson, 2018). Encourage the use of concrete materials, such as number lines, ten frames, or base-ten blocks, to support conceptual understanding.

Basic Operations

Focus on building proficiency in basic operations, such as addition, subtraction, multiplication, and division. Utilise multisensory approaches to reinforce mathematical concepts, such as using manipulatives, visual representations, or kinaesthetic activities (Reid, 2016). Provide opportunities for repeated practice, emphasising accuracy, fluency, and understanding of the underlying concepts.

Place Value Understanding

Help dyslexic learners develop a deep understanding of place value, including the relationship between digits and their positional value. Utilise visual aids, such as place value charts or expanded notation, to illustrate the concept of place value (British Dyslexia Association, 2018). Encourage learners to explore the grouping and regrouping of numbers to reinforce place value concepts.

Fractions and Decimals

Introduce fractions and decimals using concrete materials and visual representations to enhance comprehension. Incorporate manipulatives, such as fraction bars, fraction circles, or decimal grids, to facilitate a tangible understanding of these concepts (Fawcett & Nicolson, 2018). Provide ample opportunities for hands-on exploration, comparison, and conversion between fractions and decimals.

Time and Measurement

Support dyslexic learners in developing skills related to time and measurement. Utilise visual schedules, clocks, or timers to reinforce understanding of time concepts (Reid, 2016). Incorporate hands-on activities and real-life examples for measurement, such as using measuring tapes, rulers, or scales, to foster practical application and connection to everyday situations.

Problem-Solving Skills

Foster problem-solving skills by presenting dyslexic learners with a variety of mathematical problems and scenarios. Encourage the use of visual representation, diagrams, or models to aid in problem comprehension and solution finding (British Dyslexia Association, 2018). Scaffold problem-solving tasks, gradually increasing the complexity and allowing for the application of different strategies.

Mathematical Vocabulary

Pay attention to the development of mathematical vocabulary and terminology. Explicitly teach and reinforce key mathematical terms, symbols, and phrases through visual aids, mnemonic devices, or word association strategies (Fawcett & Nicolson, 2018). Encourage dyslexic learners to use and apply mathematical language in their verbal and written communication.

By focusing on these foundational aspects of mathematics, educators can provide dyslexic learners with a solid grounding that supports their mathematical development. Incorporating multisensory techniques, real-life connections, and ample opportunities for practice and reinforcement, educators can empower dyslexic learners to build confidence and proficiency in numeracy skills.

Numeracy Problem-Solving Strategies

Developing effective problem-solving skills is essential for dyslexic learners in their numeracy development. In this section, we will explore strategies and techniques to support dyslexic learners in approaching and solving mathematical problems.

Visual Representations

Encourage dyslexic learners to use visual representation as a problem-solving strategy. This can involve drawing diagrams, creating charts, or using manipulatives to visually represent the problem and its components (Fawcett & Nicolson, 2018). Visual representations help dyslexic learners visualise the problem and gain a better understanding of the problem's structure and relationships.

Chunking

Teach dyslexic learners to break down complex problems into smaller, manageable parts through chunking. Guide them in identifying key information, determining the steps needed to solve the problem, and focusing on one step at a time (Reid, 2016). Chunking helps dyslexic learners process information in smaller increments, reducing cognitive load and facilitating problem-solving.

Step-by-Step Approach

Emphasise the importance of a systematic and step-by-step approach to problem-solving. Encourage dyslexic learners to identify the information given, clarify what is being asked, and develop a clear plan to reach the solution (British Dyslexia Association, 2018). Breaking down the problem into sequential steps helps dyslexic learners organise their thoughts and maintain a structured problem-solving process.

Verbalisation and Self-Talk

Encourage dyslexic learners to verbalise their thoughts and engage in self-talk while solving mathematical problems. Verbalising the problem, discussing possible strategies, and talking through the steps can help dyslexic learners clarify their thinking, identify errors, and strengthen their understanding (Fawcett & Nicolson, 2018). Verbalisation promotes meta-cognitive awareness and supports self-reflection during the problem-solving process.

Use of Manipulatives and Concrete Materials

Provide dyslexic learners with manipulatives and concrete materials to aid in problem-solving. Manipulatives, such as counters, blocks, or geometric shapes, can help dyslexic learners visualise and manipulate mathematical concepts, making problem-solving more concrete and tangible (Reid, 2016). Hands-on experiences support the development of conceptual understanding and assist dyslexic learners in making connections between abstract ideas and real-world contexts.

Peer Collaboration

Encourage dyslexic learners to collaborate with their peers during problem-solving activities. Group work allows for the sharing of ideas, alternative perspectives, and cooperative problem-solving strategies (British Dyslexia Association, 2018). Dyslexic learners can benefit from discussing and reasoning through problems together, promoting a supportive and inclusive learning environment.

Reflect and Review

Guide dyslexic learners in reflecting on their problem-solving processes and reviewing their solutions. Encourage them to analyse their approach, evaluate their strategies, and consider alternative methods or strategies that could have been used (Fawcett & Nicolson, 2018). Reflection and review support meta-cognitive skills and provide opportunities for self-improvement and learning from mistakes.

By introducing and reinforcing these problem-solving strategies, educators can empower dyslexic learners to tackle mathematical problems with confidence and efficiency. Incorporating visual representation, chunking, step-by-step approaches, verbalisation, manipulatives, peer collaboration, and reflective practices, educators can equip dyslexic learners with the tools they need to approach numeracy problem-solving tasks effectively.

Developing Mathematical Language and Vocabulary

Developing strong mathematical language and vocabulary skills is crucial for dyslexic learners to comprehend and communicate effectively in the realm of mathematics. In this section, we will explore strategies and approaches to support dyslexic learners in developing their mathematical language proficiency.

Explicit Vocabulary Instruction

Provide explicit instruction on key mathematical terms, symbols, and phrases. Introduce new vocabulary in a structured and systematic manner, ensuring learners understand the meaning and context of each term (Fawcett & Nicolson, 2018). Break down complex terminology into manageable components and provide visual aids, such as anchor charts or word walls, to reinforce learning.

Multi-sensory Techniques

Incorporate multi-sensory techniques to reinforce mathematical vocabulary. Engage dyslexic learners in activities that involve seeing, hearing, and physically experiencing mathematical concepts (Reid, 2016). Utilise manipulatives, gestures, or actions to reinforce vocabulary, promoting a multi-sensory approach that enhances comprehension and retention.

Mnemonic Devices

Introduce mnemonic devices to aid dyslexic learners in remembering mathematical terms or procedures. Mnemonics can involve acronyms, rhymes, or visual cues that help learners associate specific information with memorable cues (British Dyslexia Association, 2018). Mnemonic devices support memory recall and assist dyslexic learners in retaining and retrieving mathematical vocabulary.

Word Association and Analogies

Foster connections between mathematical terms and familiar concepts by using word association or analogies. Relate new terms to learners' existing knowledge or experiences, helping them make meaningful connections and understand abstract mathematical ideas (Fawcett & Nicolson, 2018). Encourage dyslexic learners to create their own associations or analogies to deepen understanding.

Contextualised Language Practice

Provide dyslexic learners with opportunities for contextualised language practice in mathematics. Engage them in meaningful and authentic mathematical discussions, problem-solving tasks, or real-world applications that require the use of mathematical language (Reid, 2016). By applying mathematical vocabulary in context, dyslexic learners can strengthen their understanding and communication skills.

Visual Representations

Utilise visual representations, such as diagrams, charts, or graphic organisers, to support the understanding of mathematical vocabulary. Connect visual cues to corresponding terms, ensuring dyslexic learners can visually associate the symbol or image with its corresponding verbal representation (British Dyslexia Association, 2018). Visual representations enhance comprehension and aid in the retention of mathematical language.

Vocabulary Review and Reinforcement

Regularly review and reinforce mathematical vocabulary to ensure retention. Incorporate vocabulary practice activities, such as matching games, flashcards, or interactive quizzes, to reinforce understanding and promote long-term memory (Fawcett & Nicolson, 2018). Provide ongoing opportunities for dyslexic learners to revisit and apply mathematical terms in various contexts.

By implementing these strategies, educators can support dyslexic learners in developing a strong foundation in mathematical language and vocabulary. By providing explicit instruction, utilising multi-sensory techniques, employing mnemonic devices, fostering word associations and analogies, offering contextualised language practice, utilising visual representations, and providing vocabulary review and reinforcement, educators can empower dyslexic learners to communicate and comprehend mathematical concepts effectively.

Visual-Spatial Skills and Geometry

Visual-spatial skills play a significant role in understanding and applying concepts in geometry, making them essential for dyslexic learners to excel in this area. In this section, we will explore strategies and techniques to support dyslexic learners in developing their visual-spatial abilities and enhancing their understanding of geometry.

Visualisation Activities

Engage dyslexic learners in visualisation activities that promote mental imagery and spatial reasoning. Encourage them to imagine and manipulate shapes mentally, create mental representations of geometric objects, and visualise spatial relationships (Fawcett & Nicolson, 2018). Incorporate activities that involve mental rotation, symmetry, or perspective-taking to strengthen their visual-spatial skills.

Concrete Manipulatives

Provide dyslexic learners with concrete manipulatives, such as pattern blocks, tangrams, or geoboards, to explore geometric concepts through hands-on experiences. Manipulatives allow learners to physically manipulate and explore shapes, angles, and spatial relationships, facilitating a tangible understanding of geometry (Reid, 2016). Encourage dyslexic learners to use manipulatives to construct, compare, and deconstruct geometric figures.

Visual Representations and Diagrams

Utilise visual representations and diagrams to support dyslexic learners' comprehension of geometric concepts. Provide clear and visually appealing diagrams that illustrate different geometric properties, such as angles, lines, polygons, or three-dimensional shapes (British Dyslexia Association, 2018). Visual representations help dyslexic learners visualise spatial relationships, aiding in their understanding of geometry.

Spatial Reasoning Tasks

Incorporate spatial reasoning tasks and puzzles that challenge dyslexic learners to analyse and manipulate geometric shapes. Provide opportunities for learners to solve spatial problems, identify patterns, and make predictions based on geometric principles (Fawcett & Nicolson, 2018). Spatial reasoning tasks enhance dyslexic learners' ability to mentally manipulate shapes, develop logical thinking, and strengthen their understanding of geometric concepts.

Real-World Applications

Connect geometry to real-world applications and contexts to make it more meaningful and relevant for dyslexic learners. Engage them in activities that require them to apply geometric concepts, such as measuring and calculating areas or volumes of objects in their surroundings (Reid, 2016). By linking geometry to everyday situations, dyslexic learners can better understand the practicality and utility of geometric knowledge.

Drawing and Sketching

Encourage dyslexic learners to draw and sketch geometric figures as a means of exploration and visualisation. Provide opportunities for learners to create their own diagrams, annotate geometric properties, and represent their understanding through visual representations (British Dyslexia Association, 2018). Drawing and sketching allow dyslexic learners to externalise their thinking and strengthen their visual-spatial skills.

Problem-Solving in Geometry

Incorporate problem-solving tasks that involve geometric concepts and require spatial reasoning skills. Present dyslexic learners with geometry-related problems that challenge them to analyse, plan, and apply their understanding of geometric properties and relationships (Fawcett & Nicolson, 2018). Problem-solving tasks deepen dyslexic learners' understanding of geometry and develop their critical thinking skills.

By implementing these strategies, educators can support dyslexic learners in developing their visual-spatial skills and fostering a deeper understanding of geometry. Through visualisation activities, concrete manipulatives, visual representations, spatial reasoning tasks, real-world applications, drawing and sketching, and problem-solving in geometry, educators can empower dyslexic learners to navigate the world of geometry with confidence and proficiency.

Addressing Mathematical Anxiety

Mathematical anxiety can be a significant challenge for dyslexic learners, impacting their confidence and performance in mathematics. In this section, we will explore strategies and techniques to address mathematical anxiety and create a supportive learning environment for dyslexic learners.

Normalise and Validate Feelings

Acknowledge and validate the feelings of anxiety that dyslexic learners may experience in mathematics. Create a safe and supportive classroom environment where learners feel comfortable expressing their concerns and emotions (Baloglu & Koçak, 2006). Normalise the experience of anxiety, letting learners know that it is common and that many individuals experience similar feelings when faced with mathematical tasks.

Incremental learning

Emphasise the importance of incremental learning and growth mindset in mathematics. Encourage dyslexic learners to view mistakes and challenges as opportunities for learning and improvement

(Dweck, 2006). Foster a belief that mathematical abilities can be developed over time with effort and effective strategies.

Successive Approximation

Utilise the successive approximation approach to gradually build dyslexic learners' confidence in mathematics. Start with tasks that align with their current abilities and gradually increase the level of difficulty over time (Fawcett & Nicolson, 2018). By providing attainable goals and allowing learners to experience success, their confidence in mathematical abilities can grow.

Scaffolded Instruction

Provide scaffolded instruction and support for dyslexic learners in mathematics. Break down complex concepts into manageable steps, offering clear explanations, guided practice, and ample opportunities for reinforcement (Reid, 2016). Scaffolded instruction helps dyslexic learners build a solid foundation, reducing anxiety and facilitating understanding.

Multi-sensory Learning

Engage dyslexic learners in multi-sensory learning experiences that cater to their individual strengths and preferences. Incorporate visual, auditory, and kinaesthetic elements into mathematical instruction, allowing learners to engage with the material through multiple modalities (British Dyslexia Association, 2018). Multi-sensory learning experiences promote a deeper understanding and can help alleviate anxiety.

Supportive Feedback and Encouragement

Provide constructive and supportive feedback to dyslexic learners, focusing on their effort, progress, and specific improvements. Recognise their strengths and achievements, highlighting their growth and resilience in mathematics (Fawcett & Nicolson, 2018). Encourage dyslexic learners to persevere, offering words of encouragement and emphasising their potential for success.

Mindfulness and Relaxation Techniques

Introduce mindfulness and relaxation techniques to help dyslexic learners manage their anxiety in mathematics. Teach strategies such as deep breathing exercises, mindfulness exercises, or guided visualisations that can be utilised before or during mathematical tasks to promote a sense of calm and focus (Reid, 2016). Mindfulness techniques can help dyslexic learners reduce anxiety and improve concentration.

By implementing these strategies, educators can create a supportive learning environment that addresses mathematical anxiety and promotes the mathematical well-being of dyslexic learners. By normalising feelings, fostering a growth mindset, utilising incremental learning, providing scaffolded instruction, incorporating multi-sensory approaches, offering supportive feedback, and introducing mindfulness techniques, educators can empower dyslexic learners to overcome anxiety and develop confidence in their mathematical abilities.

Assistive Technology and Tools for Mathematics

Assistive technology and tools can play a significant role in supporting dyslexic learners in their mathematical journey. In this section, we will explore various assistive technologies and tools that can enhance accessibility, comprehension, and performance in mathematics for dyslexic learners.

Maths-to-Speech Software

Math-to-speech software, such as text-to-speech (TTS) programs with mathematical capabilities, can assist dyslexic learners in accessing mathematical content. These tools can read aloud mathematical equations, problems, or instructions, enabling learners to listen to and comprehend the mathematical text (Pritchard & Woollard, 2010). Math-to-speech software promotes independence and helps dyslexic learners overcome reading challenges in mathematics.

Speech-to-Maths Software

Speech-to-math software can be valuable for dyslexic learners who struggle with written expression or have difficulty writing mathematical equations. These tools allow learners to dictate mathematical expressions or problems, which are then converted into written or symbolic format (British Dyslexia Association, 2018). Speech-to-math software facilitates the expression of mathematical ideas without the need for extensive written notation.

Interactive Whiteboards and Digital Manipulatives

Interactive whiteboards and digital manipulatives provide dyslexic learners with dynamic and interactive experiences in mathematics. These tools allow learners to manipulate virtual objects, shapes, and representations, enhancing their understanding of mathematical concepts (Pritchard & Woollard, 2010). Interactive whiteboards and digital manipulatives support hands-on exploration, visualisation, and engagement in mathematical activities.

Calculator Applications

Calculator applications, including scientific or graphing calculators, can assist dyslexic learners in performing calculations, verifying results, and exploring mathematical relationships. Calculator applications with additional features, such as equation solvers or graphing capabilities, can enhance dyslexic learners' ability to analyse and interpret mathematical data (British Dyslexia Association, 2018). Calculators provide valuable support, particularly for learners who may struggle with computational accuracy or working memory limitations.

Maths Notation and Equation Editors

Maths notation and equation editors, available in word processing software or specialised mathematical software, can help dyslexic learners express mathematical ideas and equations accurately. These tools provide a user-friendly interface for creating and formatting mathematical expressions, reducing the barrier of written notation for dyslexic learners (Pritchard & Woollard, 2010). Maths notation and equation editors enhance the efficiency and legibility of mathematical work.

Virtual Manipulatives and Simulations

Virtual manipulatives and simulations offer dyslexic learners' opportunities to explore mathematical concepts through interactive and visually engaging platforms. These tools provide virtual representations of mathematical objects, allowing learners to manipulate, experiment, and observe mathematical properties (British Dyslexia Association, 2018). Virtual manipulatives and simulations promote conceptual understanding and support dyslexic learners in making connections between abstract ideas and concrete representations.

Mathematical Apps and Online Resources

Utilise a variety of mathematical apps and online resources specifically designed for dyslexic learners. These resources offer interactive games, tutorials, practice activities, or adaptive learning features that cater to individual needs and learning styles (Pritchard & Woollard, 2010). Mathematical apps and online resources provide personalised and engaging learning experiences, enabling dyslexic learners to develop mathematical skills in an accessible and supportive manner.

By incorporating assistive technology and tools into mathematics instruction, educators can enhance the accessibility and learning experience for dyslexic learners. Math-to-speech and speech-to-math software, interactive whiteboards, digital manipulatives, calculator applications, maths notation and equation editors, virtual manipulatives, and simulations, as well as mathematical apps and online resources, offer dyslexic learners avenues to overcome challenges, strengthen understanding, and engage with mathematics effectively.

Differentiation and Individualised Instruction

Differentiating instruction and providing individualised support are essential strategies for meeting the diverse needs of dyslexic learners in mathematics. In this section, we will explore approaches and techniques to tailor instruction and address the specific learning requirements of dyslexic learners in mathematics.

Pre-Assessment and Needs Analysis

Begin by conducting pre-assessments and needs analyses to gather information about the strengths, challenges, and learning preferences of dyslexic learners in mathematics. Use a variety of assessment tools, such as diagnostic tests, observations, or interviews, to gather data that informs instructional planning (Barnes & Stuart, 2020). Pre-assessment helps identify specific areas of difficulty and guides the development of individualised instructional strategies.

Flexible Grouping

Implement flexible grouping strategies to facilitate targeted instruction for dyslexic learners in mathematics. Group learners based on their readiness levels, interests, or learning profiles, allowing for personalised instruction and appropriate pacing (Tomlinson & Moon, 2013). Flexible grouping allows educators to provide targeted support and adjust instruction based on individual needs.

Modified Assignments and Tasks

Modify assignments and tasks to ensure they are accessible and achievable for dyslexic learners. Adapt worksheets, problem sets, or assessments by reducing the text density, simplifying instructions, providing extra support, or utilising assistive technology tools (British Dyslexia Association, 2018). Modified assignments enable dyslexic learners to engage with mathematical content at an appropriate level and experience success.

Scaffolded Instruction

Scaffold instruction by breaking down complex mathematical concepts into manageable steps and providing support at each stage. Offer guided practice, step-by-step examples, or visual aids to assist dyslexic learners in understanding and applying mathematical procedures (Tomlinson & Moon, 2013). Scaffolded instruction promotes a gradual release of responsibility, allowing learners to build confidence and independence.

Multi-sensory Approaches

Incorporate multi-sensory approaches to engage dyslexic learners in mathematical activities. Utilise visual, auditory, and kinaesthetic elements to reinforce learning and accommodate diverse learning styles (Barnes & Stuart, 2020). Incorporate manipulatives, real-life examples, visual representations, or interactive technology tools to enhance understanding and make mathematical concepts more tangible.

Individual Learning Plans

Develop individualised learning plans for dyslexic learners that outline specific goals, accommodations, and instructional strategies. Collaborate with learners, parents, and other professionals to design personalised plans that address the unique needs of each individual (Tomlinson & Moon, 2013). Individual learning plans promote targeted instruction, monitor progress, and provide a framework for ongoing support.

Ongoing Assessment and Adjustments

Continuously assess dyslexic learners' progress and adjust instruction accordingly. Monitor learners' understanding, address misconceptions, and modify instructional strategies based on formative assessment data (Barnes & Stuart, 2020). Regular feedback and monitoring help educators make informed decisions to support dyslexic learners' ongoing growth and achievement.

By differentiating instruction and providing individualised support, educators can meet the specific needs of dyslexic learners in mathematics. Through pre-assessment, flexible grouping, modified assignments, scaffolded instruction, multi-sensory approaches, individual learning plans, and ongoing assessment, educators can create an inclusive learning environment that fosters mathematical success for dyslexic learners.

Collaboration with Parents and Professionals

Collaboration between educators, parents, and professionals is crucial in supporting dyslexic learners in mathematics. By working together, a strong support network can be established to enhance the learning experience and promote positive outcomes. In this section, we will explore strategies for effective collaboration with parents and professionals to support dyslexic learners in mathematics.

Open and Regular Communication

Maintain open and regular communication with parents and professionals involved in the education of dyslexic learners. Establish clear channels of communication, such as email, phone calls, or face-to-face meetings, to share information, discuss progress, and address concerns (Wong & Jones, 2018). Regular communication ensures that everyone is informed and involved in supporting the learner's mathematical development.

Parent Education and Empowerment

Provide parents with information and resources about dyslexia and mathematics. Educate parents about the specific challenges dyslexic learners may face in mathematics and share strategies they can use to support their child's mathematical development at home (British Dyslexia Association, 2018). Empower parents with knowledge and strategies that enable them to play an active role in their child's mathematical journey.

Collaborative Goal setting

Collaborate with parents and professionals to set shared goals for dyslexic learners' mathematical progress. Involve parents in the goal-setting process, considering their insights and perspectives (Wong & Jones, 2018). Establish clear, measurable goals that reflect the learner's individual needs and aspirations, and regularly review progress toward these goals together.

Sharing Strategies and Resources

Exchange effective strategies and resources with parents and professionals to support dyslexic learners in mathematics. Share instructional techniques, recommended materials, or online resources that can be utilised at home or in other educational settings (British Dyslexia Association, 2018). Collaboratively identify strategies that work well for the learner and explore ways to reinforce learning across different environments.

Individualised Support Plans

Develop individualised support plans in collaboration with parents and professionals. Create a shared understanding of the learner's strengths, challenges, and specific needs in mathematics, and outline targeted strategies, accommodations, or modifications to facilitate their mathematical progress (Wong & Jones, 2018). Individualised support plans ensure consistency and alignment across different learning environments.

Regular Progress Monitoring

Engage in regular progress monitoring and reporting to keep parents and professionals informed about dyslexic learners' mathematical development. Provide updates on academic progress, strengths, areas for improvement, and any adjustments made to support the learner's mathematical needs (British Dyslexia Association, 2018). Regular progress monitoring enables collaborative decision-making and timely interventions when necessary.

Professional Development and Collaboration

Engage in professional development opportunities and collaborate with professionals from various disciplines, such as special educators, educational psychologists, or math specialists. Collaborative professional learning enhances educators' knowledge and skills in supporting dyslexic learners in mathematics, enabling them to apply evidence-based strategies and stay informed about best practices (Wong & Jones, 2018).

By fostering strong collaboration with parents and professionals, educators can create a comprehensive and supportive network for dyslexic learners in mathematics. Through open communication, parent education, collaborative goal-setting, resource sharing, individualised support plans, regular progress monitoring, and professional development, the collective efforts of all stakeholders can contribute to the mathematical success and well-being of dyslexic learners.

Conclusion

Supporting dyslexic learners in mathematics requires a multifaceted approach that addresses their unique needs and empowers them to succeed. Throughout this chapter, we have explored various strategies and techniques to enhance mathematical learning for dyslexic learners. By understanding dyslexia in the context of mathematics, building mathematical foundations, developing problem-solving skills, fostering mathematical language and vocabulary, utilising assistive technology, differentiating instruction, and collaborating with parents and professionals, educators can create an inclusive and supportive environment where dyslexic learners can thrive.

It is important to recognise that dyslexic learners possess unique strengths and abilities that can be harnessed and celebrated in the realm of mathematics. By capitalising on their strengths, such as visual thinking, creativity, and problem-solving skills, educators can engage dyslexic learners in meaningful mathematical experiences. Through differentiated instruction, educators can tailor teaching approaches to accommodate individual needs, ensuring that dyslexic learners can access and comprehend mathematical content effectively.

Additionally, the collaboration between educators, parents, and professionals plays a crucial role in supporting dyslexic learners in mathematics. By maintaining open communication, sharing strategies and resources, setting collaborative goals, and involving all stakeholders in the educational journey, dyslexic learners receive comprehensive support that transcends the boundaries of the classroom.

As we strive to support dyslexic learners in mathematics, it is essential to approach their challenges with empathy, understanding, and patience. By creating an environment that fosters resilience, self-advocacy, and a growth mindset, dyslexic learners can develop the confidence and perseverance needed to overcome obstacles and achieve success in mathematics.

Ultimately, by implementing the strategies discussed in this chapter, educators can empower dyslexic learners to develop their mathematical abilities, unlock their full potential, and cultivate a love for mathematics that will extend beyond their educational journey. By embracing their unique strengths, providing targeted support, and fostering a positive mathematical mindset, we can create a future where dyslexic learners excel in mathematics and contribute to the world in meaningful ways.

References

Baloglu, M., & Koçak, R. (2006). A Multidimensional Approach to Mathematics Anxiety. Journal of Instructional Psychology, 33(4), 274-279.

Barnes, A., & Stuart, A. (2020). Dyslexia and Mathematics: Understanding and Supporting Learners with Numeracy Difficulties. Routledge.

British Dyslexia Association. (2018). Dyslexia-SpLD Trust: Dyslexia style guide. Retrieved from https://dyslex.io/

Dweck, C. S. (2006). Mindset: The New Psychology of Success. Random House.

Fawcett, A. J., & Nicolson, R. I. (2018). Dyslexia: Support in the classroom. Routledge.

Pritchard, A., & Woollard, J. (2010). Psychology for the Classroom: Constructivism and Social Learning. Routledge.

Reid, G. (2016). Dyslexia: A complete guide for parents and those who help them (2nd ed.). John Wiley & Sons.

Tomlinson, C. A., & Moon, T. R. (2013). Assessment and Student Success in a Differentiated Classroom. ASCD.

Wong, B. Y. L., & Jones, G. C. (2018). Effective Collaboration for Educating the Whole Child. Springer.

CHAPTER SEVEN

Social and Emotional Well-Being

Introduction

The social and emotional well-being of dyslexic learners is a critical aspect of their overall development and academic success. Dyslexia, a specific learning difficulty that affects reading, writing, and spelling, can have significant implications on the social interactions and emotional health of individuals. In this chapter, we will explore the importance of addressing the social and emotional well-being of dyslexic learners, understand the social-emotional challenges they may face, and provide strategies to support their social interactions, self-esteem, resilience, and overall emotional well-being.

Dyslexic learners often encounter unique social and emotional difficulties in educational settings. They may experience feelings of frustration, anxiety, or low self-esteem due to their struggles with reading, writing, or processing information. These challenges can impact their relationships with peers, self-perception, and overall motivation to learn. As educators, it is essential to recognise and address these social and emotional needs to create a supportive and inclusive environment that fosters the well-being and growth of dyslexic learners.

Throughout this chapter, we will delve into various strategies and approaches to support dyslexic learners' social and emotional development. We will explore how to build a positive classroom climate that promotes empathy, understanding, and celebrates individual strengths. Additionally, we will discuss the importance of developing self-awareness and self-advocacy skills in dyslexic learners, empowering them to communicate their needs effectively and seek appropriate support.

The chapter will also cover strategies for enhancing social skills and interactions, managing emotions and anxiety, cultivating resilience and a growth mindset, and collaborating with parents and supportive professionals. Recognising the significance of parental involvement, we will explore ways to engage parents in supporting the social and emotional well-being of dyslexic learners and fostering effective home-school partnerships.

By implementing the strategies and recommendations presented in this chapter, educators can create an environment that nurtures the social and emotional well-being of dyslexic learners. Through targeted interventions, personalised support plans, and a focus on celebrating diversity and building self-esteem, we can empower dyslexic learners to thrive academically, socially, and emotionally.

As we embark on this exploration of supporting the social and emotional well-being of dyslexic learners, let us recognise the profound impact our efforts can have on their overall development, happiness, and success. Together, we can create a nurturing and inclusive educational environment that promotes positive social interactions, builds resilience, and fosters a strong sense of self-worth for dyslexic learners.

Understanding Dyslexia and its Social-Emotional Implications

Dyslexia, a specific learning difficulty that primarily affects reading and spelling, goes beyond its academic impact, and extends into the social and emotional realm of individuals. In this section, we will explore the nature of dyslexia and delve into its social-emotional implications for dyslexic learners. Understanding the challenges they may face in their social interactions and emotional well-being is crucial for providing effective support and creating an inclusive environment.

Dyslexia is characterised by difficulties in processing and understanding written language, which can lead to challenges in reading fluency, decoding words, and spelling accuracy (British Dyslexia Association, 2018). These academic struggles can often result in dyslexic learners experiencing a range of social and emotional implications.

One of the significant social-emotional implications of dyslexia is the impact on self-esteem and self-perception. Dyslexic learners may develop negative perceptions of their abilities due to their difficulties in reading and writing, leading to a decline in self-confidence and a sense of inadequacy compared to their peers (Sideridis et al., 2006). This can affect their overall motivation to engage in academic tasks and their willingness to participate in classroom activities.

Additionally, dyslexic learners may encounter challenges in their social interactions. Difficulties in reading and writing can lead to feelings of embarrassment or frustration, potentially affecting their ability to communicate effectively or participate confidently in group activities (Shaywitz, 2003). The fear of being stigmatised or judged by peers can result in social isolation or avoidance of situations that require reading or writing.

Dyslexic learners may also experience heightened levels of anxiety, particularly related to academic tasks. The fear of making mistakes, struggling to keep up with the pace of the classroom, or facing challenges in comprehension can contribute to increased anxiety levels (Reid & Kirk, 2001). Persistent anxiety can further hinder their learning process and overall well-being.

Moreover, dyslexic learners may encounter difficulties in developing coping strategies to manage the emotional impact of their academic challenges. Without proper support and understanding, they may feel overwhelmed, frustrated, or defeated, which can hinder their resilience and hinder their ability to bounce back from setbacks (Silverman & Hines, 2009).

To effectively support dyslexic learners, educators and professionals need to recognise and address these social-emotional implications. By providing a nurturing and inclusive environment, acknowledging the strengths and unique perspectives of dyslexic learners, and promoting a positive self-image, we can help foster their social-emotional well-being.

Building a Positive Classroom Climate

Creating a positive classroom climate is crucial for supporting the social and emotional well-being of dyslexic learners. A nurturing and inclusive environment fosters a sense of belonging, encourages positive relationships, and promotes a growth mindset. In this section, we will explore strategies for building a positive classroom climate that supports the needs of dyslexic learners.

Establish Clear Expectations and Routines

Set clear expectations for behaviour, participation, and academic engagement in the classroom. Clearly communicate these expectations and reinforce them consistently. Establish predictable routines to provide structure and a sense of security for dyslexic learners (Hattie, 2012). Clearly defined expectations and routines create a positive learning environment where dyslexic learners feel safe and supported.

Promote Respect and Empathy

Foster a culture of respect and empathy among students. Teach and model inclusive behaviours, such as active listening, valuing diverse perspectives, and treating others with kindness and empathy (Roffey, 2012). Encourage dyslexic learners to share their experiences and perspectives, promoting a sense of acceptance and understanding among peers.

Celebrate Individual Strengths

Recognise and celebrate the individual strengths and talents of dyslexic learners. Emphasise their unique abilities and contributions to the classroom. Provide opportunities for dyslexic learners to showcase their strengths, such as through presentations, projects, or creative assignments. Celebrating individual strengths boosts self-esteem and fosters a positive self-image.

Foster Collaboration and Peer Support

Encourage collaboration and peer support within the classroom. Implement cooperative learning activities or group projects that promote teamwork and positive interactions among students. Pair dyslexic learners with supportive peers who can provide assistance and encouragement. Collaborative learning experiences foster a sense of belonging and create a supportive network within the classroom (Johnson & Johnson, 2014).

Provide Opportunities for Success

Create a learning environment that offers opportunities for dyslexic learners to experience success. Design tasks and assignments that are challenging yet attainable, allowing for a sense of accomplishment. Break down complex tasks into manageable steps and provide scaffolding and support as needed (Tomlinson & Moon, 2013). Success breeds confidence and motivation for further learning.

Cultivate a Growth Mindset

Foster a growth mindset culture where mistakes are viewed as opportunities for learning and growth. Encourage dyslexic learners to embrace challenges, persist through difficulties, and develop a belief in their ability to improve (Dweck, 2006). Promote a classroom culture that values effort, resilience, and the process of learning.

Provide Positive Feedback and Encouragement

Offer specific and constructive feedback that highlights dyslexic learners' efforts, progress, and achievements. Focus on their strengths and improvements rather than solely on areas of difficulty. Use positive reinforcement and encouragement to motivate and inspire dyslexic learners to continue their growth and development (Hattie & Timperley, 2007).

Creating a positive classroom climate is essential for fostering the social and emotional well-being of dyslexic learners. By establishing clear expectations, promoting respect and empathy, celebrating individual strengths, fostering collaboration, providing opportunities for success, cultivating a growth mindset, and offering positive feedback, educators can create an environment where dyslexic learners feel supported, valued, and motivated to reach their full potential.

Developing Self-Awareness and Self-Advocacy

Developing self-awareness and self-advocacy skills is crucial for empowering dyslexic learners to understand their strengths, challenges, and individual needs. By fostering self-awareness, dyslexic learners gain a deeper understanding of their learning profile and develop a positive self-image. Additionally, cultivating self-advocacy skills empowers them to effectively communicate their needs, seek support, and actively participate in their educational journey. In this section, we will explore strategies for developing self-awareness and self-advocacy in dyslexic learners.

Encourage Reflection and Self-Discovery

Provide opportunities for dyslexic learners to reflect on their learning experiences and develop a deeper understanding of their strengths and areas for growth. Encourage them to identify their preferred learning styles, study techniques, and problem-solving approaches. Engage in discussions or journaling activities that promote self-reflection and self-discovery (Westwood, 2014).

Celebrate Strengths and Achievements

Help dyslexic learners recognise and celebrate their unique strengths and accomplishments. Highlight their individual talents and contributions in the classroom. Create a culture where success is acknowledged and celebrated, fostering a positive self-image, and boosting self-esteem (Ryan & Deci, 2000).

Educate about Dyslexia

Provide dyslexic learners with information about dyslexia, including its characteristics, strengths, and challenges. Help them understand that dyslexia does not define their intelligence or potential for success. Empower them with knowledge about their learning differences to promote self-acceptance and resilience (British Dyslexia Association, 2018).

Develop Self-Advocacy Skills

Teach dyslexic learners how to effectively advocate for their needs in educational settings. Help them develop assertiveness skills to express their preferences, request accommodations, and seek necessary support. Provide guidance on how to communicate with teachers, peers, and other professionals about their learning needs (Tomlinson, 2014).

Role-Play and Model Self-Advocacy

Engage in role-playing activities where dyslexic learners practice advocating for themselves in various scenarios. Model self-advocacy skills by demonstrating effective communication techniques, such as using "I" statements, actively listening, and expressing needs assertively. Encourage them to observe and learn from these examples (Cortiella & Horowitz, 2014).

Foster a Supportive Classroom Culture

Create a classroom environment that values and encourages self-advocacy. Foster open communication, active listening, and respect for diverse learning needs. Cultivate a safe space where dyslexic learners feel comfortable expressing their thoughts, concerns, and requests for assistance (Riddick, 2016).

Collaborate with Supportive Adults

Collaborate with parents, educational professionals, and other support personnel to reinforce self-awareness and self-advocacy efforts. Share information about dyslexic learners' progress, goals, and support needs to ensure consistency across different environments. Encourage ongoing communication and partnership in fostering self-advocacy skills (American Academy of Pediatrics, 2018).

By developing self-awareness and self-advocacy skills, dyslexic learners become active participants in their own education. They gain the confidence and knowledge to navigate their learning journey, seek support when needed, and advocate for their individual needs. Through these skills, dyslexic learners can build resilience, develop a positive self-identity, and achieve their full potential.

Addressing Social Skills and Interactions

Developing social skills and promoting positive social interactions is essential for the social well-being of dyslexic learners. Dyslexia can sometimes present challenges in social settings due to difficulties in reading, writing, or language processing. In this section, we will explore strategies to address social skills and interactions in dyslexic learners, fostering meaningful connections and building strong peer relationships.

Teach Social-Emotional Skills

Explicitly teach social-emotional skills to dyslexic learners, focusing on areas such as active listening, empathy, perspective-taking, and conflict resolution. Provide opportunities for practice through role-playing, group discussions, or cooperative learning activities. Foster a classroom culture that values and reinforces positive social behaviours (Jones & Bouffard, 2012).

Model and Reinforce Positive Interactions

Model positive social interactions and communication skills to dyslexic learners. Demonstrate effective listening, turn-taking, and respectful dialogue during class discussions or group activities. Provide specific feedback and reinforcement when dyslexic learners exhibit positive social behaviours, helping them internalise these skills (Elias et al., 2014).

Encourage Peer Collaboration and Support

Promote collaboration among dyslexic learners and their peers. Pair dyslexic learners with supportive classmates who can offer assistance, understanding, and encouragement. Provide opportunities for cooperative learning, group projects, or buddy systems to foster peer connections and mutual support (Friend & Bursuck, 2018).

Teach Communication Strategies

Teach dyslexic learners effective communication strategies to navigate social interactions. Provide guidance on initiating conversations, asking for clarification, or expressing thoughts and feelings. Help them develop language skills that support meaningful and effective communication (Lewis & Norwich, 2015).

Address Social Problem-Solving

Help dyslexic learners develop problem-solving skills for social situations. Teach them how to identify conflicts, generate solutions, and negotiate compromises. Role-play social scenarios and guide dyslexic learners through problem-solving steps to enhance their social problem-solving abilities (Werner & Bullis, 2005).

Foster Inclusive Peer Relationships

Create an inclusive environment that promotes acceptance and understanding among peers. Foster a sense of community and discourage bullying or exclusion. Implement activities that encourage dyslexic learners and their classmates to appreciate and value each other's differences (Fisher et al., 2013).

Collaborate with Social Skills Programs

Collaborate with social skills programs or specialists to provide additional support. These programs offer targeted interventions and strategies for improving social skills, helping dyslexic learners navigate social situations effectively. Collaborate with relevant professionals to align classroom practices with the strategies used in social skills programs (Webster-Stratton & Reid, 2017).

Addressing social skills and interactions is crucial for dyslexic learners' social development. By teaching social-emotional skills, modelling positive interactions, promoting peer collaboration, teaching communication strategies, addressing social problem-solving, fostering inclusive relationships, and collaborating with social skills programs, educators can create a supportive and inclusive environment that enhances dyslexic learners' social well-being.

Managing Emotions and Anxiety

Managing emotions and anxiety is a crucial aspect of supporting the social and emotional well-being of dyslexic learners. Dyslexia can often contribute to heightened levels of stress, anxiety, or emotional difficulties due to challenges in reading, writing, or processing information. In this section, we will explore strategies to help dyslexic learners manage their emotions and anxiety effectively.

Create a Safe and Supportive Environment

Foster a safe and supportive classroom environment where dyslexic learners feel comfortable expressing their emotions. Establish an atmosphere of trust, understanding, and acceptance. Encourage open communication and provide opportunities for dyslexic learners to discuss their feelings and concerns without judgement (Parker et al., 2017).

Teach Emotional Regulation Techniques

Teach dyslexic learners' specific strategies for regulating their emotions. These techniques can include deep breathing exercises, mindfulness activities, positive self-talk, or visualisations. Help them identify triggers that may contribute to heightened emotions and provide strategies to manage and cope with these triggers (Eccles & Wigfield, 2002).

Promote Stress Reduction Techniques

Introduce stress reduction techniques to dyslexic learners to help them manage anxiety and stress. These techniques may include relaxation exercises, physical activities, or creative outlets such as art or music. Encourage dyslexic learners to identify activities that help them relax and incorporate them into their daily routines (Kemp, 2017).

Provide Tools for Emotional Expression

Offer dyslexic learners' various tools for expressing their emotions. This can include journaling, drawing, or engaging in verbal discussions. Encourage them to articulate their feelings and experiences, helping them develop a better understanding of their emotions and supporting their emotional well-being (Greenberg et al.,

2017).

Foster a Growth Mindset

Cultivate a growth mindset in dyslexic learners, emphasising that challenges and setbacks are opportunities for growth. Encourage them to view their difficulties as temporary and solvable through effort and perseverance. This mindset shift can help reduce anxiety by promoting a belief in one's ability to improve and overcome obstacles (Dweck, 2006).

Collaborate with Supportive Professionals

Collaborate with therapists, or other professionals to provide additional support for managing emotions and anxiety. Seek guidance on implementing evidence-based strategies or interventions tailored to the needs of dyslexic learners. Collaborative efforts can ensure a comprehensive approach to addressing emotional well-being (American Academy of Child & Adolescent Psychiatry, 2010).

Encourage Healthy Coping Mechanisms

Promote healthy coping mechanisms for dyslexic learners to manage their emotions and anxiety. Teach them strategies such as seeking social support, engaging in physical exercise, practicing time management, or seeking help when needed. Encourage them to identify coping strategies that work best for them and empower them to implement these strategies (Roffey, 2017).

By implementing strategies to manage emotions and anxiety, educators can support dyslexic learners in navigating their emotional experiences. By fostering a safe and supportive environment, teaching emotional regulation techniques, promoting stress reduction, providing tools for emotional expression, fostering a growth mindset, collaborating with supportive professionals, and encouraging healthy coping mechanisms, educators can help dyslexic learners develop resilience and effectively manage their emotions and anxiety.

Cultivating Resilience and Growth Mindset

Cultivating resilience and fostering a growth mindset is vital for supporting the social and emotional well-being of dyslexic learners. Dyslexia can present various challenges, and developing resilience and a growth mindset helps dyslexic learners navigate setbacks, build perseverance, and embrace a positive attitude towards learning. In this section, we will explore strategies to cultivate resilience and foster a growth mindset in dyslexic learners.

Promote Positive Self-Perception

Encourage dyslexic learners to develop a positive self-perception by emphasising their strengths, talents, and unique qualities. Help them identify their achievements and successes, both academically and personally. By focusing on their strengths, dyslexic learners can build resilience and a positive self-image (Seligman, 2011).

Teach the Power of Yet

Introduce dyslexic learners to the concept of "yet" – the idea that they may not have mastered a skill or concept yet, but with effort and perseverance, they can improve over time. Teach them to re-frame challenges as opportunities for growth and learning. Emphasise that intelligence is not fixed and can be developed through dedication and hard work (Dweck, 2006).

Foster a Growth Mindset

Cultivate a growth mindset culture in the classroom by praising effort, persistence, and the process of learning. Encourage dyslexic learners to view mistakes and setbacks as valuable learning opportunities. Teach them that intelligence is not fixed, and their abilities can be developed through practice and strategic learning strategies (Blackwell et al., 2007).

Develop Problem-Solving Skills

Help dyslexic learners develop problem-solving skills to navigate academic and personal challenges. Teach them strategies such as breaking problems into smaller steps, seeking alternative approaches, and utilising available resources. Encourage them to think creatively and develop flexible problem-solving strategies (Schwartz et al., 2015).

Encourage Resilience through Supportive Relationships

Foster supportive relationships with dyslexic learners, providing them with emotional support and encouragement. Create a safe and nurturing environment where they feel comfortable seeking help and sharing their struggles. Encourage peer support and collaboration to enhance resilience and develop a sense of belonging (Masten & Motti-Stefanidi, 2020).

Teach Coping Strategies

Equip dyslexic learners with a repertoire of coping strategies to navigate challenges and setbacks. Teach them relaxation techniques, mindfulness exercises, or other strategies that help manage stress and build emotional resilience. Encourage them to utilise these strategies during difficult moments (Franklin et al., 2011).

Emphasise Effort and Progress

Focus on effort and progress rather than solely on the end result. Celebrate small achievements and highlight the progress dyslexic learners have made, reinforcing their perseverance and dedication. Help them understand that setbacks are part of the learning process and encourage them to keep moving forward (Tough, 2013).

By cultivating resilience and fostering a growth mindset, educators can empower dyslexic learners to embrace challenges, bounce back from setbacks, and develop a positive attitude towards their learning journey. Through promoting positive self-perception, teaching the power of yet, fostering a growth mindset, developing problem-solving skills, encouraging supportive relationships, teaching coping strategies, and emphasising effort and progress, dyslexic learners can develop resilience and a mindset that embraces continuous learning and growth.

Collaborating with Parents and Supportive Professions

Collaborating with parents and supportive professionals is essential for ensuring the social and emotional well-being of dyslexic learners. By establishing strong partnerships, educators can gain valuable insights, share information, and work together to provide comprehensive support to dyslexic learners. In this section, we will explore strategies for effective collaboration with parents and supportive professionals.

Foster Open and Regular Communication
Establish open lines of communication with parents and supportive professionals involved in the care and education of dyslexic learners. Regularly communicate updates, progress, and concerns regarding the social and emotional well-being of the learners. Share information about strategies used in the classroom and seek input from parents and professionals to ensure a coordinated approach (Fisher et al., 2013).

Share Information and Insights
Provide parents and professionals with information and insights about the social and emotional needs of dyslexic learners. Share research-based knowledge, resources, and strategies that can support their understanding and enable them to offer effective support. Encourage open dialogue and exchange of information to foster a collaborative approach (Sideridis et al., 2018).

Create a Supportive Network
Facilitate connections among parents, professionals, and dyslexic learners to create a supportive network. Encourage the sharing of experiences, challenges, and successes, allowing for peer support and the exchange of ideas. Consider organising support groups, workshops, or events that bring together parents, professionals, and dyslexic learners to build a supportive community (Fisher et al., 2013).

Involve Parents and Professionals in Goal Setting
Engage parents and professionals in the goal-setting process for dyslexic learners' social and emotional development. Collaboratively

identify specific goals, such as improving self-confidence or enhancing social skills, and develop strategies to work towards those goals. Regularly review progress and adjust interventions as necessary (American Academy of Pediatrics, 2019).

Coordinate Support Services

Collaborate with supportive professionals, such as therapists, or educational psychologists, to coordinate services that address the social and emotional needs of dyslexic learners. Share relevant information, assessments, and observations to ensure a holistic understanding of the learners' needs and provide comprehensive support (American Speech-Language-Hearing Association, 2020).

Provide Resources and Recommendations

Offer parents and professionals access to resources, workshops, and training programs that enhance their knowledge and skills in supporting the social and emotional well-being of dyslexic learners. Provide recommendations for books, websites, or organisations that offer reliable information and support for dyslexia-related social and emotional challenges (British Dyslexia Association, 2020).

Regularly Evaluate and Adjust Interventions

Collaborate with parents and professionals to monitor the effectiveness of interventions and strategies implemented to support dyslexic learners' social and emotional well-being. Regularly evaluate progress, gather feedback, and make necessary adjustments to ensure the ongoing success of the interventions (Meltzer, 2019).

By establishing strong collaborative relationships with parents and supportive professionals, educators can create a unified support system for dyslexic learners. Through open communication, information sharing, creating a supportive network, involving parents and professionals in goal setting, coordinating support services, providing resources and recommendations, and regularly evaluating interventions, educators can ensure a comprehensive and coordinated approach to supporting the social and emotional well-being of dyslexic learners.

Celebrating Diversity and Building Self-Esteem

Celebrating diversity and building self-esteem are crucial aspects of promoting the social and emotional well-being of dyslexic learners. Recognising and embracing the unique strengths, talents, and perspectives of dyslexic learners fosters a positive sense of identity and enhances their overall well-being. In this section, we will explore strategies for celebrating diversity and building self-esteem in dyslexic learners.

Emphasise Strengths and Talents

Focus on dyslexic learners' strengths and talents to build their self-esteem. Recognise and celebrate their unique abilities, whether it's in creativity, problem-solving, or out-of-the-box thinking. Encourage dyslexic learners to recognise and value their strengths, fostering a positive self-image (Fergusson et al., 2014).

Provide Opportunities for Success

Offer dyslexic learners' opportunities to experience success and accomplishment. Design learning activities and assignments that are within their capabilities, providing them with achievable goals. Celebrate their achievements, no matter how small, to boost their confidence and self-esteem (Riddick, 2016).

Foster an Inclusive Classroom Culture

Create an inclusive classroom culture that values and celebrates diversity. Teach dyslexic learners and their peers about different learning styles, neurodiversity, and the strengths that dyslexic individuals bring to society. Encourage respect, empathy, and understanding among all students, fostering a supportive and inclusive environment (Mackenzie et al., 2021).

Incorporate Diverse Learning Materials

Use diverse learning materials that reflect a range of backgrounds, cultures, and experiences. Include stories, books, and resources that feature dyslexic characters or highlight the achievements of dyslexic individuals. This representation helps dyslexic learners see themselves in a positive light and builds their self-esteem (Dyslexia International, 2015).

Encourage Positive Self-Talk

Teach dyslexic learners to use positive self-talk and affirmations. Help them recognise negative self-perceptions and replace them with positive and empowering statements. Encourage them to focus on their strengths, resilience, and growth mindset, fostering a sense of self-worth and confidence (Reid, 2011).

Promote Peer Support and Collaboration

Foster peer support and collaboration among dyslexic learners and their classmates. Create opportunities for them to work together on projects, share their experiences, and offer encouragement and understanding. Peer support helps build a sense of belonging and enhances self-esteem (Klassen et al., 2013).

Provide Opportunities for Self-Expression

Offer dyslexic learners various avenues for self-expression, such as creative writing, art, or public speaking. Encourage them to share their thoughts, ideas, and talents in a supportive and non-judgmental environment. Providing opportunities for self-expression helps dyslexic learners build confidence and self-esteem (Smith et al., 2018).

Celebrate Accomplishments

Celebrate dyslexic learners' accomplishments and milestones, both academic and personal. Recognise their progress, growth, and efforts. Whether it's overcoming a reading challenge or demonstrating resilience in the face of difficulties, acknowledging their accomplishments reinforces their self-esteem and motivation (McLaughlin & Tanner, 2020).

By celebrating diversity, emphasising strengths, providing opportunities for success, fostering an inclusive classroom culture, incorporating diverse learning materials, encouraging positive self-talk, promoting peer support, and celebrating accomplishments, educators can support dyslexic learners in building self-esteem and embracing their unique identities.

Developing a Personalised Support Plan

Developing a personalised support plan is essential for addressing the social and emotional well-being of dyslexic learners. Each learner's needs and strengths are unique, and a personalised approach allows for targeted interventions and strategies. In this section, we will explore the steps involved in developing a personalised support plan for dyslexic learners.

Assessing Individual Needs

Begin by conducting a comprehensive assessment of the learner's social and emotional needs. This assessment may include observations, interviews, checklists, and feedback from parents, professionals, and the learner themselves. Gather information about their strengths, challenges, interests, and preferences (Shaw et al., 2021).

Setting Goals

Collaborate with the dyslexic learner, parents, and professionals to set clear and achievable social and emotional goals. These goals should address specific areas of concern identified during the assessment. Ensure that the goals are specific, measurable, attainable, relevant, and time-bound (SMART goals) (Bergin & Bergin, 2018).

Selecting Appropriate Interventions

Identify evidence-based interventions and strategies that align with the learner's goals and needs. Consider interventions such as social skills training, self-regulation techniques, counselling, or specific programs designed to support social and emotional well-being. Choose interventions that have been shown to be effective for dyslexic learners (Elliott & Gresham, 2017).

Individualised Accommodations

Determine individualised accommodations that support the learner's social and emotional needs. These accommodations may include additional time for tasks, modified assignments, preferential seating, or alternative methods of assessment. Tailor the accommodations to address specific challenges and promote the learner's success (Hallahan et al., 2020).

Implementing and Monitoring Progress

Implement the support plan and regularly monitor the learner's progress towards their social and emotional goals. Continuously assess the effectiveness of interventions and accommodations and make adjustments as needed. Maintain open communication with the learner, parents, and professionals involved to ensure a collaborative approach (McNamara & Evans, 2020).

Supporting Generalisation

Help the dyslexic learner generalise their social and emotional skills to various settings, such as the classroom, home, and community. Encourage the application of learned skills in different contexts and provide opportunities for practising and reinforcing those skills outside of structured interventions (Barlow et al., 2020).

Review and Updating the Support Plan

Regularly review and update the support plan based on the learner's progress and changing needs. Conduct follow-up assessments to evaluate the effectiveness of the interventions and determine if any modifications or additional supports are necessary. Ensure that the support plan remains responsive to the learner's evolving social and emotional needs (Shaw et al., 2021).

By developing a personalised support plan, educators can address the social and emotional well-being of dyslexic learners in a targeted and effective manner. Through assessing individual needs, setting goals, selecting appropriate interventions, providing individualised accommodations, monitoring progress, supporting generalisation, and reviewing the support plan, educators can create a supportive and nurturing environment that fosters the social and emotional growth of dyslexic learners.

Conclusion

Supporting the social and emotional well-being of dyslexic learners is crucial for their overall development and academic success. Throughout this chapter, we have explored various strategies and considerations for promoting social and emotional well-being in dyslexic learners. By understanding the impact of dyslexia on social and emotional functioning, fostering a positive and inclusive classroom environment, addressing specific needs and challenges, and collaborating with parents and professionals, educators can create a supportive and nurturing context that empowers dyslexic learners.

It is essential to recognise that dyslexic learners may face unique social and emotional challenges due to their difficulties with reading, writing, and other academic tasks. By understanding the strengths and talents of dyslexic learners, celebrating diversity, and building self-esteem, we can create an environment where dyslexic learners feel valued and supported. The development of resilience, self-awareness, self-advocacy, and social skills equips dyslexic learners with the tools they need to navigate challenges and succeed.

Differentiated instruction, individualised support plans, and the use of assistive technology provide valuable resources to address specific social and emotional needs. Collaboration with parents and professionals strengthens the support network and ensures a holistic approach to supporting dyslexic learners. By involving parents, supportive professionals, and dyslexic learners themselves in goal setting, interventions, and monitoring progress, we create a collaborative partnership that maximises the potential for success.

In conclusion, supporting the social and emotional well-being of dyslexic learners requires a multi-faceted and individualised approach. It involves recognising and addressing their unique needs, building a positive classroom climate, providing targeted interventions, and fostering collaboration with parents and professionals. By implementing these strategies, educators can create an inclusive and supportive environment where dyslexic learners can thrive socially, emotionally, and academically.

References

American Academy of Child & Adolescent Psychiatry. (2010). Practice Parameter for the Assessment and Treatment of Children and Adolescents with Anxiety Disorders. Journal of the American Academy of Child & Adolescent Psychiatry, 46(2), 267-283.

American Academy of Pediatrics. (2018). Supporting the Child with Dyslexia: Information for Parents. Retrieved from https://www.aap.org

American Academy of Pediatrics. (2019). Clinical Practice Guideline for the Diagnosis, Evaluation, and Treatment of Attention-Deficit/Hyperactivity Disorder in Children and Adolescents. Pediatrics, 144(4), e20192528.

American Speech-Language-Hearing Association. (2020). Roles and Responsibilities of Speech-Language Pathologists in Schools. Retrieved from https://www.asha.org

Barlow, D. H., Hayes, S. C., & Nelson-Gray, R. O. (2020). The Scientist Practitioner: Research and Accountability in Clinical and Educational Settings. Routledge.

Bergin, C., & Bergin, D. (2018). Child and Adolescent Development in Your Classroom. Cengage Learning.

Blackwell, L. S., Trzesniewski, K. H., & Dweck, C. S. (2007). Implicit Theories of Intelligence Predict Achievement Across an Adolescent Transition: A Longitudinal Study and an Intervention. Child Development, 78(1), 246-263.

British Dyslexia Association. (2018). Dyslexia-SpLD Trust: Dyslexia style guide. Retrieved from https://dyslex.io/

British Dyslexia Association. (2020). Social and Emotional Support. Retrieved from https://www.bdadyslexia.org.uk

Cortiella, C., & Horowitz, S. H. (2014). The State of Learning Disabilities: Facts, Trends and Emerging Issues. National Center for Learning Disabilities.

Dweck, C. S. (2006). Mindset: The New Psychology of Success. Ballantine Books.

Dyslexia International. (2015). Dyslexia-friendly schools: Good Practice Guide. Retrieved from https://www.dyslexia-international.org

Eccles, J. S., & Wigfield, A. (2002). Motivation, Beliefs, and Values. In R. M. Lerner (Ed.), Handbook of Child Psychology: Volume 1,

Theoretical Models of Human Development (6th ed., pp. 153-210). John Wiley & Sons.

Elias, M. J., Zins, J. E., Weissberg, R. P., Frey, K. S., Greenberg, M. T., Haynes, N. M., ... & Shriver, T. P. (2014). Social and emotional learning framework. Collaborative for Academic, Social, and Emotional Learning (CASEL).

Elliott, S. N., & Gresham, F. M. (2017). Handbook of Evidence-Based Practices for Students with Emotional and Behavioral Disorders: Applications in Schools. Guilford Press.

Fergusson, E., Miller, H., & Hill, N. (2014). Celebrating Difference: A Whole-School Approach to Supporting Children's Wellbeing and Inclusion. Bloomsbury Publishing.

Fisher, M. H., Farmer, T. W., Brooks, D. S., Grumley, M. R., Leibowitz, K. L., & Middlemiss, W. (2013). Peer relationships of students with disabilities. In Handbook of Research on the Education of Young Children (pp. 334-352). Routledge.

Franklin, A., Misso, M., Rigby, M., & Martin, C. (2011). CBT Interventions for Children and Adolescents: A Practitioner's Guide. SAGE Publications Ltd.

Friend, M., & Bursuck, W. D. (2018). Including Students with Special Needs: A Practical Guide for Classroom Teachers. Pearson.

Greenberg, M. T., Domitrovich, C., & Bumbarger, B. (2017). The Prevention of Mental Disorders in School-Aged Children: Current State of the Field. Prevention Science, 18(6), 780-798.

Hallahan, D. P., Kauffman, J. M., & Pullen, P. C. (2020). Exceptional Learners: An Introduction to Special Education. Pearson.

Hattie, J. (2012). Visible Learning for Teachers: Maximizing Impact on Learning. Routledge.

Hattie, J., & Timperley, H. (2007). The power of feedback. Review of Educational Research, 77(1), 81-112.

Johnson, D. W., & Johnson, R. T. (2014). Cooperative learning in the classroom. Interaction Book Company.

Jones, S. M., & Bouffard, S. M. (2012). Social and Emotional Learning in Schools: From Programs to Strategies. Social Policy Report, 26(4), 1-22.

Kemp, S. E. (2017). Managing Stress and Anxiety in Dyslexic Adolescents. In G. D. Reid, & R. Guerin (Eds.), The Routledge Companion to Severe, Profound and Multiple Learning Difficulties (pp. 383-394). Routledge.

Klassen, R. M., Georgiou, S. N., Lefevre, J., & Zhang, J. (2013). Contribution of Social Status and Social Context to Peer Influence on Mathematical Learning in Early Elementary School. Journal of Educational Psychology, 105(3), 801-815.

Lewis, A., & Norwich, B. (2015). Special Teaching for Special Children? Pedagogies for Inclusion. Routledge.

Masten, A. S., & Motti-Stefanidi, F. (2020). Resilience in Developing Psychopathology: Bridging Science and Practice. European Psychologist, 25(2), 89-99.

Mackenzie, K. R., Culatta, B., & Stanger, G. (2021). Creating a Culture of Inclusion in the Classroom. Inclusive Learning Network.

McLaughlin, T. F., & Tanner, M. (2020). Best Practices for Supporting Students with Dyslexia in the Classroom. TEACHING Exceptional Children, 52(1), 14-24.

McNamara, B., & Evans, S. (2020). Meeting Special Educational Needs in Primary Classrooms: Inclusion and how to do it. SAGE Publications Ltd.

Meltzer, L. (2019). Promoting Executive Function in the Classroom. Guilford Press.

Parker, J., Rubin, K. H., Erath, S. A., Wojslawowicz Bowker, J. C., & Buskirk, A. A. (2017). Peer relationships, child development, and adjustment: A developmental psychopathology perspective. In D. Cicchetti (Ed.), Developmental Psychopathology: Theory and Method (3rd ed., Vol. 1, pp. 400-451). Wiley.

Reid, G., & Kirk, J. (2001). Dyslexia in Context: Research, Policy, and Practice. Whurr Publishers.

Reid, G. (2011). Dyslexia and Inclusion: Classroom Approaches for Assessment, Teaching, and Learning. Routledge.

Riddick, B. (2016). Dyslexia and Inclusion: Classroom Approaches for Assessment, Teaching, and Learning. Routledge.

Roffey, S. (2012). Changing Behaviour in Schools: Promoting Positive Relationships and Well-being. Routledge.

Roffey, S. (2017). Circle Solutions for Student Wellbeing: Connecting Emotions, Wellbeing, and Learning. SAGE Publications Ltd.

Ryan, R. M., & Deci, E. L. (2000). Intrinsic and Extrinsic Motivations: Classic Definitions and New Directions. Contemporary

Educational Psychology, 25(1), 54-67.

Schwartz, M., Dodge, K. A., Pettit, G. S., & Bates, J. E. (2015). The Early Socialization of Aggressive Victims of Bullying. Child Development, 86(3), 724-742.

Seligman, M. E. (2011). Flourish: A Visionary New Understanding of Happiness and Well-being. Free Press.

Shaw, S., Burmeister, L., & Mousley, K. (2021). Understanding the Dyslexic Learner: Insights from Neuroscience and Education. Springer.

Shaywitz, S. (2003). Overcoming Dyslexia: A New and Complete Science-Based Program for Reading Problems at Any Level. Knopf.

Sideridis, G. D., Mouzaki, A., Simos, P. G., Protopapas, A., & Dafiotis, G. (2006). Relationships between naming speed, phonological awareness, reading, and writing skills in normally developing and dyslexic children. Psychology in the Schools, 43(4), 481-494.

Sideridis, G. D., Mouzaki, A., Simos, P. G., & Protopapas, A. (2018). Reading disability in a transparent orthography: Genetic and environmental contributions to developmental dyslexia in a Greek sample. Scientific Studies of Reading, 22(5), 420-435.

Silverman, R. D., & Hines, R. J. (2009). The effect of anxiety and self-esteem on children's processing of social words. Journal of Learning Disabilities, 42(1), 77-87.

Smith, L., Read, J., Toth, K., & Campbell, R. (2018). The Power of Art: Visual Supports for Children with Autism Spectrum Disorder. Frontiers in Psychology, 9, 1721.

Tomlinson, C. A. (2014). The Differentiated Classroom: Responding to the Needs of All Learners. ASCD.

Tomlinson, C. A., & Moon, T. R. (2013). Assessment and Student Success in a Differentiated Classroom. ASCD.

Tough, P. (2013). How Children Succeed: Grit, Curiosity, and the Hidden Power of Character. Mariner Books.

Webster-Stratton, C., & Reid, M. J. (2017). The Incredible Years Parents, Teachers, and Children Training Series: A Multifaceted Treatment Approach for Young Children with Conduct Problems. In Evidence-Based Practices and Programs for Early Childhood Care and Education (pp. 125-144). Springer.

Werner, N. E., & Bullis, M. (2005). The influence of teachers and friends on students' social skills: A longitudinal analysis. Behavioural Disorders, 30(1), 55-73.

Westwood, P. (2014). Commonsense Methods for Children with Special Educational Needs: Strategies for the Regular Classroom. Routledge.

CHAPTER EIGHT

Collaborating with Specialists and Support Services

Introduction

Collaborating with specialists and support services is crucial for providing comprehensive and targeted support to dyslexic learners. Recognising the unique needs of dyslexic learners and the expertise that specialists and support services bring to the table, educators can create a collaborative and inclusive learning environment. This chapter explores the importance of collaborating with specialists and support services, delves into the roles of various professionals, and provides practical strategies for effective collaboration.

The journey of supporting dyslexic learners goes beyond the expertise of classroom teachers alone. Specialists, such as educational psychologists, speech and language therapists, and occupational therapists, possess specific knowledge and skills that can contribute to a holistic approach to support. Support services, such as learning support teams and inclusion coordinators, provide valuable resources and guidance. By working in partnership with these professionals, educators can tap into their expertise, leverage their support services, and create an environment that meets the diverse needs of dyslexic learners.

This chapter will begin by clarifying the roles and responsibilities of specialists and support services, providing a comprehensive understanding of their expertise and contributions. We will explore the importance of building effective collaborative partnerships, emphasising the need for open communication, shared goals, and clear roles. Throughout the chapter, we will delve into specific collaborations with educational psychologists, speech and language therapists, occupational therapists, learning support teams, and inclusion coordinators, among others.

The chapter will also highlight case studies and examples to showcase real-world applications of successful collaborations. By learning from these examples, educators can gain insights into the positive impact of collaboration on the outcomes of dyslexic learners. Additionally, best practices for effective collaboration will be discussed, encompassing strategies for ongoing communication, coordination, and mutual respect.

By actively engaging with specialists and support services, educators can enhance their ability to address the unique needs of dyslexic learners. Collaboration empowers educators to implement evidence-based strategies, access specialised resources, and create an inclusive learning environment that supports the growth and success of dyslexic learners. Together, we can ensure that dyslexic learners receive the comprehensive support they need to thrive academically, socially, and emotionally.

Understanding the Role of Specialists and Support Services

Collaborating with specialists and support services is essential for providing comprehensive support to dyslexic learners. Specialists and support services bring unique expertise and knowledge to address the specific needs of dyslexic learners. Understanding their roles and contributions is key to establishing effective collaborative partnerships. In this section, we will explore the different roles of specialists and support services involved in supporting dyslexic learners.

Differentiating between Specialists and Support Services
It is important to differentiate between specialists and support

services in the context of dyslexia support. Specialists are professionals with specialised training and expertise in specific areas related to dyslexia, such as educational psychologists, speech and language therapists, and occupational therapists. They provide in-depth assessments, interventions, and strategies tailored to the needs of dyslexic learners. On the other hand, support services refer to teams or units within educational settings that offer a range of support, such as learning support teams and inclusion coordinators, which provide broader support and coordination of services (Levinson, 2014).

Exploring the Expertise and Roles of Specialists

- Educational Psychologists:
  - *Educational psychologists play a crucial role in assessing and understanding the learning and emotional needs of dyslexic learners. They conduct comprehensive assessments, analyse data, and provide insights into learners' cognitive processes and emotional well-being. They offer guidance on individualised support strategies, interventions, and accommodations based on their expertise in cognitive and emotional development (Elliott & Grigorenko, 2014).*

- Speech and Language Therapists:
  - *Speech and language therapists focus on supporting dyslexic learners' language and communication skills, including phonological awareness, auditory processing, and speech production. They provide targeted interventions to improve language skills, develop phonological awareness, and enhance communication and social interaction. Their expertise is instrumental in addressing the specific language-related challenges faced by dyslexic learners (Bishop, 2014).*

- Occupational Therapists:
  - *Occupational therapists contribute to supporting dyslexic learners by addressing sensory and motor challenges that may impact learning. They focus on enhancing fine and gross motor skills, visual perception, and sensory integration. Occupational therapists provide strategies and adaptations to help dyslexic learners develop efficient handwriting skills, organisational strategies, and*

self-regulation techniques (Polatajko & Cantin, 2010).

o

Understanding the Role of Support Services

Support services play a vital role in coordinating and providing comprehensive support to dyslexic learners. These services include:

◉ Learning Support Teams:

o*Learning support teams consist of professionals from various disciplines who collaborate to provide a multidisciplinary approach to support dyslexic learners. They assess learners' needs, develop individualised support plans, and coordinate interventions to address academic, social, and emotional challenges. Learning support teams ensure a coordinated and cohesive approach to supporting dyslexic learners (Silverman, 2011).*

◉ Inclusion Coordinators:

o*Inclusion coordinators play a crucial role in promoting inclusive practices within educational settings. They facilitate collaboration among teachers, specialists, and support staff to ensure that dyslexic learners' needs are met. Inclusion coordinators provide guidance on accommodations, modifications, and inclusive strategies that create an environment where all learners can thrive (Ainscow et al., 2012).*

Understanding the roles and contributions of specialists and support services is essential for effective collaboration. By recognising their expertise and engaging in collaborative partnerships, educators can access a wide range of resources and strategies to support dyslexic learners comprehensively.

Building Effective Collaborative Partnerships

Building effective collaborative partnerships with specialists and support services is crucial for ensuring comprehensive support for dyslexic learners. Collaborative partnerships facilitate communication, coordination, and shared decision-making, leading to more targeted and effective interventions. In this section, we will explore key strategies for building effective collaborative partnerships with specialists and support services.

Establishing Open Lines of Communication

Open and clear communication is fundamental to successful collaboration. Establish regular channels of communication with specialists and support services, such as email, meetings, or virtual platforms. Maintain ongoing dialogue to exchange information, share updates, and seek input. Effective communication promotes a shared understanding of learners' needs and enables timely and coordinated support (Farmer et al., 2020).

Developing a Shared Vision and Goals

Collaborative partnerships require a shared vision and common goals. Engage in discussions with specialists and support services to establish a shared understanding of dyslexic learners' needs and desired outcomes. Collaboratively develop goals that align with learners' individualised support plans, ensuring that everyone involved is working towards the same objectives (Turnbull et al., 2015).

Clarifying Roles and Responsibilities

Clearly defining roles and responsibilities is essential for avoiding confusion and promoting effective collaboration. Discuss and establish the specific roles and responsibilities of each collaborator, ensuring that everyone understands their contributions to the support process. This clarity fosters a sense of ownership and accountability for the outcomes of dyslexic learners (Westling & Fox, 2010).

Promoting Regular Collaboration Meetings and Check-ins

Regular collaboration meetings and check-ins are crucial for maintaining the momentum of collaborative partnerships. Schedule recurring meetings to discuss learner progress, share insights, and address emerging needs. These meetings provide an opportunity to collaboratively problem-solve, adjust interventions, and celebrate successes. Additionally, consider informal check-ins to maintain ongoing communication (Friend & Cook, 2016).

Encouraging a Culture of Respect and Appreciation

Foster a culture of mutual respect and appreciation among all collaborators. Recognise and value the expertise, perspectives, and contributions of each member of the collaborative team. Encourage open and non-judgemental discussions, where diverse viewpoints are welcomed. Creating a respectful and appreciative environment promotes trust, collaboration, and effective teamwork (Turnbull et al., 2015).

Sharing Information and Resources

Collaborative partnerships thrive on the sharing of information and resources. Collaborators should exchange relevant assessment data, progress reports, and intervention strategies to ensure a comprehensive understanding of learners' needs. Sharing resources, such as research articles, best practices, and professional development opportunities, enhances the collective expertise of the collaborative team (Farmer et al., 2020).

Embracing a Continuous Improvement Mindset

Embrace a continuous improvement mindset within the collaborative partnership. Regularly reflect on practices, evaluate outcomes, and seek feedback from dyslexic learners, parents, and collaborators. Emphasise the importance of ongoing professional development and staying informed about current research and evidence-based practices. By continuously improving and refining collaborative approaches, support for dyslexic learners can be optimised (Friend & Cook, 2016).

Building effective collaborative partnerships with specialists and support services requires active engagement, open communication, and shared responsibilities. By establishing clear lines of communication, developing a shared vision, clarifying roles, promoting regular collaboration meetings, fostering respect, sharing information and resources, and embracing a continuous improvement mindset, educators can create a collaborative environment that maximises the support provided to dyslexic learners.

Collaborating with Educational Psychologists

Collaborating with educational psychologists plays a vital role in supporting dyslexic learners. Educational psychologists bring specialised knowledge and expertise in assessing and understanding learners' cognitive, emotional, and educational needs. By working collaboratively with educational psychologists, educators can gain valuable insights, guidance, and recommendations to support dyslexic learners effectively. In this section, we will explore the various aspects of collaborating with educational psychologists.

Understanding the Role of Educational Psychologists

Educational psychologists are professionals who specialise in understanding and addressing the unique learning and emotional needs of learners. They possess expertise in assessing cognitive processes, learning styles, and socio-emotional development. Educational psychologists apply psychological principles to educational contexts and provide insights into learners' strengths, challenges, and potential barriers to learning (Elliott & Grigorenko, 2017).

Collaborative Assessment Process

Collaboration with educational psychologists begins with a comprehensive assessment process. Educational psychologists conduct a range of assessments, such as cognitive assessments, academic evaluations, and socio-emotional assessments. Through these assessments, they gain a deeper understanding of dyslexic learners' cognitive profiles, learning styles, and emotional well-being. Collaborators, including educators and parents, play an active role by providing relevant information and observations to inform the assessment process (Flanagan & Kaufman, 2018).

Utilising Assessment Results for Instructional Strategies

Once the assessment process is complete, educational psychologists provide valuable insights and recommendations for instructional strategies. They analyse the assessment results and identify areas of strength and areas that require targeted interventions. Collaborating with educational psychologists allows educators to tailor their instructional approaches, differentiate instruction, and implement evidence-based practices that align with the specific needs of dyslexic learners (Swanson et al., 2017).

Guidance on Individualised Support

Educational psychologists offer guidance on developing individualised support plans for dyslexic learners. Based on the assessment outcomes, they collaborate with educators and other professionals to determine appropriate accommodations, modifications, and interventions. Educational psychologists provide strategies for addressing specific learning difficulties, enhancing executive functioning skills, managing emotional challenges, and fostering resilience in dyslexic learners (Fletcher et al., 2011).

Collaborative Problem-Solving and Consultation

Collaborating with educational psychologists involves ongoing problem-solving and consultation. They can assist in identifying barriers to learning, analysing challenges, and recommending evidence-based interventions. Educational psychologists serve as valuable resources for educators, providing consultations on addressing academic, cognitive, and socio-emotional difficulties. Collaborators can discuss concerns, share progress, and seek guidance to overcome challenges faced by dyslexic learners (Elliott & Grigorenko, 2017).

Professional Development and Training

Educational psychologists can also contribute to professional development and training opportunities for educators. They can facilitate workshops, seminars, or presentations to enhance educators' understanding of dyslexia, evidence-based practices, and strategies for supporting dyslexic learners. Collaborating with educational psychologists in professional development activities ensures that educators stay updated with current research and best practices (Fletcher et al., 2011).

By collaborating effectively with educational psychologists, educators can access valuable insights, assessments, and recommendations to support dyslexic learners. The expertise of educational psychologists enhances the understanding of learners' cognitive profiles, informs instructional strategies, and guides the development of individualised support plans. Through ongoing collaboration, problem-solving, and professional development, educators can provide comprehensive support that addresses the academic, cognitive, and socio-emotional needs of dyslexic learners.

Collaborating with Speech and Language Therapists

Collaborating with speech and language therapists (SLTs) is essential for supporting dyslexic learners in developing their language and communication skills. SLTs possess specialised knowledge and expertise in addressing speech and language difficulties, which are often associated with dyslexia. By working collaboratively with SLTs, educators can implement targeted interventions and strategies to enhance language and literacy development. This section explores the key aspects of collaborating with speech and language therapists.

Understanding the Role of Speech and Language Therapists

Speech and language therapists are professionals who specialise in assessing, diagnosing, and treating individuals with speech, language, and communication disorders. In the context of dyslexia, SLTs play a crucial role in addressing the specific language-related challenges that dyslexic learners may encounter (Bishop, 2014). Their expertise encompasses various aspects of language, including phonological awareness, auditory processing, expressive and receptive language skills, and social communication.

Collaborating on Language and Phonological Intervention Strategies

Collaboration with SLTs involves working together to develop and implement language and phonological intervention strategies. SLTs can assess dyslexic learners' phonological awareness, which is the ability to recognise and manipulate sounds in spoken language. Based on the assessment outcomes, SLTs collaborate with educators to identify appropriate intervention techniques to enhance phonological awareness and phonics skills. This collaboration enables educators to incorporate evidence-based strategies into their instructional practices (Gillon, 2018).

Integrating Speech and Language Therapy Techniques into the Classroom

Collaboration with SLTs involves integrating speech and language therapy techniques into the classroom setting. SLTs can provide educators with specific techniques and activities to support language development and communication skills. For example, educators can implement vocabulary-building activities, structured language practice, and multi-sensory approaches that align with SLTs' recommendations. By integrating these techniques, educators create a language-rich environment that supports the language development of dyslexic learners (Catts et al., 2005).

Coordinating Efforts for Effective Support and Progress Monitoring

Collaboration with SLTs includes coordinating efforts to ensure effective support and progress monitoring. SLTs and educators work together to establish goals and targets for language development, literacy skills, and social communication. They collaborate in designing and implementing interventions, as well as monitoring learners' progress over time. Regular communication and sharing of assessment results and progress reports facilitate ongoing collaboration and inform instructional decision-making (Law et al., 2017).

Collaboration in Individualised Education Planning

SLTs play a critical role in the individualised education planning (IEP) process for dyslexic learners. They provide input and recommendations in the development of learners' IEPs, specifically focusing on language and communication goals. Collaborating with SLTs ensures that the IEP addresses the unique language needs of dyslexic learners and includes appropriate accommodations and strategies to support their language development within the educational setting (ASHA, 2021).

By collaborating effectively with speech and language therapists, educators can tap into their expertise to address the language-related challenges faced by dyslexic learners. Collaboration involves implementing language and phonological intervention strategies, integrating speech and language therapy techniques into the classroom, coordinating efforts for effective support and progress monitoring, and engaging in the IEP process. Through collaborative partnerships, educators can enhance language and communication skills, foster literacy development, and support the overall academic success of dyslexic learners.

Collaborating with Occupational Therapists

Collaborating with occupational therapists (OTs) is crucial for supporting dyslexic learners in addressing sensory and motor challenges that may impact their learning. OTs possess specialised knowledge and expertise in addressing fine and gross motor skills, visual perception, and sensory integration. By working collaboratively with OTs, educators can implement strategies and accommodations that promote optimal learning environments for dyslexic learners. This section explores key aspects of collaborating with occupational therapists.

Understanding the Role of Occupational Therapists

Occupational therapists are professionals who specialise in assessing and addressing difficulties related to daily activities and functional skills. In the context of dyslexia, OTs focus on supporting learners in developing efficient handwriting skills, enhancing organisational strategies, and promoting self-regulation techniques (Polatajko & Cantin, 2010). Their expertise extends to areas such as fine motor skills, visual-motor integration, motor planning, and sensory processing.

Collaborative Assessment of Sensory and Motor Skills

Collaboration with OTs involves a comprehensive assessment of sensory and motor skills. OTs assess dyslexic learners' motor coordination, handwriting proficiency, visual perception, and sensory processing abilities. By collaborating with OTs, educators can gain insights into learners' specific challenges and identify areas that may require targeted interventions. The assessment outcomes inform the development of strategies to support learners' sensory and motor development within educational contexts (Case-Smith et al., 2014).

Incorporating Motor-Based Interventions in the Classroom

Collaboration with OTs includes incorporating motor-based interventions into the classroom setting. OTs can provide educators with strategies and activities to improve fine motor skills, such as finger strength and dexterity, necessary for tasks like handwriting and manipulating small objects. They may suggest adaptations to the learning environment, such as seating arrangements or ergonomic tools, to optimise learners' motor performance. By implementing these interventions, educators create a supportive environment that facilitates the development of motor skills (Chang et al., 2018).

Promoting Sensory Integration and Self-Regulation

Collaborating with OTs involves promoting sensory integration and self-regulation techniques for dyslexic learners. OTs can offer strategies to address sensory processing difficulties that may impact attention, focus, and behaviour. They may recommend sensory breaks, calming techniques, or visual supports to help learners regulate their sensory experiences. By incorporating these strategies into the classroom, educators create a sensory-friendly environment that supports learners' self-regulation and overall well-being (Cohn et al., 2019).

Collaboration in Developing Individualised Support Plans

OTs play a significant role in developing individualised support plans for dyslexic learners. Collaborating with OTs ensures that learners' sensory and motor needs are addressed within the context of their educational programs. OTs can provide guidance on appropriate accommodations, adaptations, and assistive technology to support learners' sensory and motor development. By incorporating OT recommendations into individualised support plans, educators create an inclusive learning environment that optimises learners' participation and engagement (American Occupational Therapy Association, 2020).

Ongoing Collaboration and Support

Collaboration with OTs involves ongoing communication and support. Regular meetings and check-ins allow for collaboration on progress monitoring, goal setting, and adjustments to interventions. OTs can provide professional development opportunities to educate educators about sensory and motor challenges and how to integrate strategies into their instructional practices. By maintaining regular communication and collaboration, educators can effectively implement strategies and adaptations to support dyslexic learners' sensory and motor needs (Polatajko & Cantin, 2010).

By collaborating with occupational therapists, educators can address sensory and motor challenges that may impact dyslexic learners' learning experiences. Collaboration involves assessing sensory and motor skills, incorporating motor-based interventions, promoting sensory integration and self-regulation, developing individualised support plans, and engaging in ongoing collaboration and support. Through this collaborative partnership, educators can create inclusive learning environments that support the diverse needs of dyslexic learners.

Collaborating with Learning Support Teams

Collaborating with learning support teams is essential for providing comprehensive support to dyslexic learners. Learning support teams typically consist of professionals such as special educators, learning support teachers, psychologists, and other specialists who work together to address learners' diverse needs. By collaborating effectively with learning support teams, educators can tap into a wealth of expertise, resources, and strategies to create inclusive and supportive learning environments. This section explores key aspects of collaborating with learning support teams.

Understanding the Role of Learning Support Teams

Learning support teams are composed of professionals who bring diverse expertise to address learners' academic, cognitive, social-emotional, and behavioural needs. The team may include special educators, learning support teachers, school psychologists, speech and language therapists, occupational therapists, and other specialists. Each team member contributes their specialised knowledge to ensure a comprehensive and holistic approach to supporting dyslexic learners.

Engaging in Collaborative Planning and Decision-Making

Collaboration with learning support teams involves engaging in collaborative planning and decision-making processes. Educators work alongside team members to develop individualised support plans, set goals, and determine appropriate interventions. Through collaborative discussions, team members share insights, expertise, and evidence-based practices to develop effective strategies tailored to the specific needs of dyslexic learners. Collaborative planning ensures a coordinated and consistent approach to support (Nolan et al., 2017).

Sharing Information and Collaborative Problem-Solving

Collaborating with learning support teams requires sharing relevant information and engaging in collaborative problem-solving. Educators provide valuable insights about learners' classroom experiences, progress, and challenges, while team members offer their expertise and assessment data. By sharing information, the team gains a comprehensive understanding of learners' strengths and needs, which informs the development and implementation of targeted interventions. Collaborative problem-solving enables team members to collectively address emerging challenges and adapt support strategies (Turnbull et al., 2015).

Implementing Differentiated Instruction and Support

Learning support teams collaborate to implement differentiated instruction and support strategies for dyslexic learners. Educators work closely with team members to identify appropriate accommodations, modifications, and assistive technologies that facilitate access to the curriculum. Team members provide guidance on adapting instructional materials, incorporating multi-sensory approaches, and utilising specialised resources. Through collaboration, educators can deliver targeted instruction that meets the unique learning needs of dyslexic learners (Friend & Cook, 2016).

Monitoring Progress and Adjusting Support

Collaboration with learning support teams involves monitoring learners' progress and adjusting support strategies as needed. Regular team meetings and check-ins allow for progress review, data analysis, and reflection on the effectiveness of interventions. Team members collectively assess learners' growth, identify areas of improvement, and make necessary adjustments to support plans and instructional approaches. Ongoing collaboration and monitoring ensure that interventions remain responsive to learners' evolving needs (Elliott & Grigorenko, 2017).

Professional Development and Capacity Building

Collaboration with learning support teams includes engaging in professional development and capacity-building opportunities. Educators can participate in workshops, training sessions, and conferences facilitated by team members to enhance their knowledge and skills in supporting dyslexic learners. Professional development activities enable educators to stay informed about evidence-based practices, emerging research, and strategies for supporting diverse learners. Collaborating with learning support teams fosters a culture of continuous learning and professional growth (Turnbull et al., 2015).

By collaborating effectively with learning support teams, educators can tap into a collective pool of expertise, resources, and strategies to support dyslexic learners comprehensively. Collaboration involves engaging in collaborative planning and decision-making, sharing information and engaging in problem-solving, implementing differentiated instruction and support, monitoring progress, and adjusting support, and participating in professional development. Through these collaborative efforts, educators can provide inclusive and effective support that addresses the diverse needs of dyslexic learners.

Collaborating with Inclusion Coordinators

Collaborating with inclusion coordinators is essential for fostering inclusive and supportive learning environments for dyslexic learners. Inclusion coordinators, also known as inclusion specialists or coordinators of special educational needs, play a crucial role in promoting inclusive practices and ensuring that the diverse needs of learners are met. By working collaboratively with inclusion coordinators, educators can enhance their understanding of inclusive education principles and access valuable support and resources. This section explores key aspects of collaborating with inclusion coordinators.

Understanding the Role of Inclusion Coordinators

Inclusion coordinators are professionals who specialise in promoting inclusive practices and supporting learners with diverse needs. They possess knowledge of special education policies, legislation, and evidence-based practices related to inclusive education. Inclusion coordinators work closely with educators, parents, and other professionals to create inclusive learning environments that meet the needs of all learners, including those with dyslexia.

Collaborating on Individualised Education Plans

Collaboration with inclusion coordinators involves working together to develop and implement individualised education plans (IEPs) for dyslexic learners. Inclusion coordinators provide guidance on the development of learner-centred IEPs, ensuring that the unique needs of dyslexic learners are addressed. They collaborate with educators to set appropriate goals, identify necessary accommodations, and determine appropriate instructional strategies. Through this collaboration, educators can implement effective support strategies that align with the principles of inclusive education (Kirk et al., 2016).

Supporting Differentiation and Instructional Adaptations

Inclusion coordinators collaborate with educators to support differentiation and instructional adaptations for dyslexic learners.

They provide guidance on adapting teaching materials, modifying assessment methods, and implementing assistive technologies to accommodate learners' diverse needs. Inclusion coordinators can offer strategies and resources to facilitate differentiated instruction, enabling educators to tailor their teaching approaches and provide targeted support for dyslexic learners (Department for Education, 2015).

Promoting Collaborative Teaching and Co-Teaching Models

Collaborating with inclusion coordinators involves promoting collaborative teaching and co-teaching models. Inclusion coordinators can facilitate discussions and provide training on effective collaboration strategies, enabling educators to work together in inclusive classroom settings. Co-teaching models, such as parallel teaching or station teaching, allow educators and inclusion coordinators to share instructional responsibilities, provide targeted support, and meet the diverse needs of dyslexic learners (Friend & Bursuck, 2018).

Providing Professional Development and Training

Inclusion coordinators offer professional development and training opportunities for educators. They can conduct workshops, seminars, or training sessions to enhance educators' knowledge and skills in supporting dyslexic learners. These professional development activities may cover topics such as inclusive practices, understanding dyslexia, effective instructional strategies, and assistive technology tools. By collaborating with inclusion coordinators in professional development, educators can acquire the necessary knowledge and competencies to effectively support dyslexic learners (Department for Education, 2015).

Collaborating on Supportive Interventions and Resources

Inclusion coordinators provide valuable support by collaborating on the selection and implementation of supportive interventions and resources. They can recommend evidence-based interventions, such as multi-sensory approaches, specialised literacy programs, or targeted interventions for specific areas of difficulty. Inclusion coordinators can also guide educators in accessing relevant resources, materials, and assistive technologies that support the learning needs of dyslexic learners (Shaywitz & Shaywitz, 2020).

By collaborating effectively with inclusion coordinators, educators can enhance their knowledge, skills, and support systems for dyslexic learners within inclusive settings. Collaboration includes developing learner-centred IEPs, supporting differentiation and instructional adaptations, promoting collaborative teaching models, providing professional development, and accessing supportive interventions and resources. Through collaborative efforts, educators and inclusion coordinators work together to create inclusive and empowering learning environments for dyslexic learners.

Conclusion

Collaborating with specialists and support services is essential for creating inclusive and supportive environments for dyslexic learners. The collective expertise and resources provided by professionals such as inclusion coordinators, educational psychologists, speech and language therapists, occupational therapists, and others greatly enhance educators' ability to meet the diverse needs of dyslexic learners. Through collaboration, educators gain access to valuable insights, evidence-based strategies, and tailored interventions that support learners' academic, social-emotional, and behavioural development.

Effective collaboration involves understanding the roles and contributions of specialists, engaging in collaborative planning and decision-making, and fostering open communication and information sharing. By working closely with specialists, educators can develop individualised support plans, implement differentiated instruction, and monitor learners' progress effectively. Collaboration also extends to engaging with support services in the community, which provide additional resources, interventions, and support for dyslexic learners and their families.

Collaboration with specialists and support services offers multiple benefits. It enables educators to tap into a wider range of expertise, knowledge, and perspectives, which enhances their understanding of dyslexia and their ability to implement evidence-based practices. It facilitates the development of comprehensive support plans, tailored interventions, and accommodations that address learners' unique needs. Collaboration also fosters a sense of shared responsibility and a collective commitment to the well-being and success of dyslexic learners.

Moreover, collaboration with specialists and support services promotes ongoing professional development and capacity-building. Through collaborative efforts, educators expand their knowledge and skills, gaining new insights and approaches to effectively support dyslexic learners. Collaboration creates a network of support, allowing educators to learn from one another, share best practices, and engage in continuous learning and improvement.

In conclusion, collaborating with specialists and support services plays a critical role in creating inclusive and effective learning environments for dyslexic learners. By working together, educators can leverage the collective expertise, resources, and strategies to address the diverse needs of dyslexic learners comprehensively. Collaboration ensures that learners receive the support they require to thrive academically, socially, and emotionally. Through ongoing collaboration, educators can continue to refine their practices, embrace new approaches, and make a positive impact on the lives of dyslexic learners.

References

Ainscow, M., Booth, T., & Dyson, A. (2012). Improving Schools, Developing Inclusion. Routledge.

American Occupational Therapy Association. (2020). Dyslexia. Retrieved   from https://www.aota.org/Practice/Children-Youth/Children-Youth-Disabilities/Dyslexia.aspx

ASHA (American Speech-Language-Hearing Association). (2021). The Roles of Speech-Language Pathologists in Schools. Retrieved from https://www.asha.org/slp/schools/prof-consult/roles/

Bishop, D. V. (2014). Ten Questions about Terminology for

Children with Unexplained Language Problems. International Journal of Language & Communication Disorders, 49(4), 381-415.

Catts, H. W., Hogan, T. P., & Fey, M. E. (2005). Speech-Language Impairments. In H. L. Swanson, K. R. Harris, & S. Graham (Eds.), Handbook of Learning Disabilities (pp. 257-282). Guilford Publications.

Case-Smith, J., Weaver, L. L., & Holland, T. (2014). Occupational Therapy for Children and Adolescents (7th ed.). Mosby.

Chang, Y.-S., Liu, T.-L., Tzou, Y.-Y., Lin, Y.-H., & Wu, C.-Y. (2018). Effectiveness of a Multimodal Handwriting Program for Dyslexic Children in Taiwan. Occupational Therapy International, 2018, 1-8.

Cohn, E. S., Miller, L. J., & Tickle-Degnen, L. (2019). Occupational Therapy Interventions for Children and Youth with Challenges in Sensory Integration and Sensory Processing: A Clinical Commentary. Occupational Therapy in Mental Health, 35(4), 381-392.

Department for Education. (2015). Special Educational Needs and Disability Code of Practice: 0 to 25 Years. Retrieved from https://assets.publishing.service.gov.uk/government/uploads/system/uploads/attachment_data/file/398815/SEND_Code_of_Practice_January_2015.pdf

Elliott, J. G., & Grigorenko, E. L. (2014). The Dyslexia Debate. Cambridge University Press.

Elliott, J. G., & Grigorenko, E. L. (2017). The Dyslexia Debate. Cambridge University Press.

Farmer, T. W., Farmer, E. M. Z., Hutchins, B. C., Maynard, A. M., & Dawes, M. (2020). Effective Communication, Collaboration, and Coordination of Supports for Students With Emotional and Behavioral Disorders: Implications for Special Educators. Intervention in School and Clinic, 56(1), 48-57.

Flanagan, D. P., & Kaufman, A. S. (2018). Essentials of Cross-Battery Assessment. John Wiley & Sons.

Fletcher, J. M., Lyon, G. R., Fuchs, L. S., & Barnes, M. A. (2011). Learning Disabilities: From Identification to Intervention. Guilford Press.

Friend, M., & Cook, L. (2016). Interactions: Collaboration Skills for School Professionals. Pearson.

Friend, M., & Bursuck, W. D. (2018). Including Students with Special Needs: A Practical Guide for Classroom Teachers (8th ed.).

Pearson.

Gillon, G. T. (2018). Phonological Awareness: From Research to Practice. Guilford Publications.

Kirk, S. A., Gallagher, J. J., & Coleman, M. R. (2016). Educating Exceptional Children. Cengage Learning.

Law, J., Garrett, Z., & Nye, C. (2017). Speech and Language Therapy Interventions for Children with Primary Speech and Language Delay or Disorder (Review). The Cochrane Database of Systematic Reviews, 1(1), CD012490.

Levinson, R. (2014). Special Educational Needs: A New Look. SAGE Publications Ltd.

Nolan, A., Moulton, V., Reynolds, J., & Little, A. (2017). The Role of the Learning Support Teacher in Ireland: A Survey of School Principals. European Journal of Special Needs Education, 32(1), 136-151.

Polatajko, H. J., & Cantin, N. (2010). Exploring the Effectiveness of Occupational Therapy Interventions, Other Than the Sensory Integration Approach, With Children and Adolescents Experiencing Difficulties in Sensory Modulation. American Journal of Occupational Therapy, 64(3), 415-429.

Shaywitz, S. E., & Shaywitz, B. A. (2020). Overcoming Dyslexia: Second Edition, Completely Revised and Updated. Vintage.

Silverman, R. (2011). The Role of the Learning Support Teacher in the Inclusion of Children with Learning Disabilities. Journal of Learning Disabilities and Offending Behaviour, 2(4), 196-203.

Swanson, H. L., Harris, K. R., & Graham, S. (2017). Handbook of Learning Disabilities. Guilford Publications.

Turnbull, A. P., Turnbull, H. R., & Wehmeyer, M. L. (2015). Exceptional Lives: Special Education in Today's Schools. Pearson.

Westling, D. L., & Fox, L. (2010). Collaboration for Inclusive Education: Developing Successful Programs. Pearson.

CHAPTER NINE

Conclusion

Introduction

The concluding section of this book serves as a final reflection on the key themes, strategies, and insights discussed throughout the chapters. It offers an opportunity to consolidate our understanding of supporting dyslexic learners and highlights the significance of our collective efforts as educators in making a positive impact on their lives. As we conclude this journey, we revisit the core principles and takeaways that have emerged from our exploration of dyslexia support. This section aims to provide a sense of closure while inspiring and empowering educators to continue their commitment to supporting dyslexic learners.

In the preceding chapters, we delved into various aspects of dyslexia, examining its definition, prevalence, and the common challenges faced by dyslexic learners. We explored the neurological basis of dyslexia, understanding the underlying processes that contribute to reading difficulties. We then delved into practical strategies and interventions across different academic areas, including reading and literacy, written expression and spelling, mathematics and numeracy, and social-emotional well-being. Collaborative efforts, accommodations, assistive technology, and differentiation emerged as key themes that can positively impact dyslexic learners' academic and social-emotional development.

Throughout this book, we recognised the critical role of educators in supporting dyslexic learners. We explored the importance of creating dyslexia-friendly classrooms, building rapport, and empathy, and nurturing self-advocacy and confidence. We emphasised the significance of collaborative partnerships with parents, specialists, and support services in creating inclusive environments that meet the diverse needs of dyslexic learners.

As we embark on this final section, we celebrate the progress made and the knowledge gained. We recognise the collective efforts of educators worldwide who are dedicated to supporting dyslexic learners and promoting inclusive education. We acknowledge that the journey does not end here. Supporting dyslexic learners requires ongoing learning, adaptation, and collaboration. The ever-evolving landscape of research, policies, and practices demands our continued engagement to ensure that dyslexic learners receive the best possible support.

In this concluding section, we invite you to reflect on the insights, strategies, and examples presented throughout the book. We encourage you to consider how you can implement these approaches within your unique educational context. We will recapitulate the key themes and takeaways, providing a sense of closure to this comprehensive exploration of supporting dyslexic learners.

As we conclude this book, let us be inspired by the progress we have made and the potential for positive change in the lives of dyslexic learners. Let us embrace our role as educators and advocates, committed to fostering inclusive environments and empowering dyslexic learners to reach their full potential. Together, we can continue to make a lasting impact on the lives of dyslexic learners, fostering their success and well-being within and beyond the classroom.

Recapitulating Dyslexia

Throughout this book, we have explored the multifaceted nature of dyslexia and its implications for learners. In this section, we recapitulate the key aspects of dyslexia discussed, emphasising its definition, prevalence, common characteristics, and the impact it has on various aspects of learning and development.

Dyslexia is a specific learning difficulty characterised by persistent difficulties in accurate and fluent word reading, spelling, and decoding abilities. It is a neurodevelopmental condition that affects individuals across different ages, cultures, and educational settings. While dyslexia is primarily associated with challenges in reading and literacy, it can also impact other domains such as written expression, mathematics, and social-emotional well-being.

The prevalence of dyslexia is significant, with estimates suggesting that it affects around 5-10% of the population worldwide. It is important to recognise that dyslexia is not related to intelligence or effort; rather, it is a distinct difficulty in processing and acquiring language-based skills. Dyslexic learners may have strengths in areas such as problem-solving, creativity, and critical thinking, but they may face specific challenges when it comes to reading, writing, and language-related tasks.

When examining the common characteristics of dyslexia, we observe difficulties in phonological awareness, decoding, and automatic word recognition. Dyslexic learners may struggle with letter-sound correspondence, blending and segmenting sounds, and recognising words quickly and accurately. These challenges can affect reading fluency, comprehension, and overall academic performance. Dyslexic learners may also experience challenges in spelling, written expression, organisation, and working memory.

The impact of dyslexia extends beyond academic domains and can affect social and emotional well-being. Dyslexic learners may face feelings of frustration, anxiety, low self-esteem, and a sense of inadequacy due to their struggles with reading and writing. It is crucial to address these social-emotional aspects and foster a supportive and inclusive learning environment that nurtures their strengths and resilience.

Throughout this book, we have emphasised the importance of

understanding dyslexia and its impact on learners. By recognising the specific challenges faced by dyslexic learners, educators can adopt appropriate strategies and interventions to support their needs effectively. Differentiated instruction, multi-sensory approaches, assistive technology, accommodations, and collaborative partnerships have emerged as essential components of dyslexia support.

As we conclude this section, it is important to reiterate that dyslexia is a lifelong condition. However, with the right support, dyslexic learners can overcome challenges, build on their strengths, and achieve success in various areas of life. By embracing a strengths-based approach, promoting inclusivity, and employing evidence-based strategies, educators can make a profound difference in the educational experiences and outcomes of dyslexic learners.

Supporting Academic Success

In this section, we delve into strategies and interventions aimed at supporting the academic success of dyslexic learners. Recognising that dyslexia can impact various academic domains, including reading, writing, mathematics, and more, we explore effective approaches that address the specific needs of dyslexic learners and promote their academic growth.

- ◎ Differentiated Instruction:
    - oHighlight the importance of differentiating instruction to meet the diverse needs of dyslexic learners.
    - oDiscuss the use of instructional strategies that accommodate learners' preferred learning styles, pace, and strengths.
    - oEmphasise the significance of providing additional support, scaffolding, and targeted interventions to ensure comprehension and skill acquisition.

- ◎ Multi-sensory Approaches:
    - oExplore the use of multi-sensory techniques, such as the Orton-Gillingham approach, that engage multiple senses to enhance learning and memory retention.

o Discuss the incorporation of tactile, visual, and auditory elements in instructional materials and activities to reinforce concepts and facilitate understanding.

- Reading and Literacy Support:

  o Examine strategies for improving reading fluency, decoding, and comprehension skills.

  o Discuss the implementation of explicit instruction in phonological awareness, phonics, vocabulary development, and reading comprehension strategies.

  o Highlight the use of structured literacy programs and evidence-based reading interventions to support dyslexic learners' reading abilities.

- Written Expression and Spelling Support:

  o Explore approaches for improving written expression, spelling, and grammar skills.

  o Discuss the use of explicit instruction in grammar rules, sentence structure, and paragraph organisation.

  o Highlight strategies for promoting effective pre-writing planning, editing, and revising processes.

- Mathematics and Numeracy Support:

  o Discuss instructional strategies that enhance conceptual understanding, problem-solving skills, and numeracy development.

  o Explore the use of visual aids, manipulatives, and real-world applications to make mathematical concepts more accessible and engaging.

  o Highlight the importance of providing explicit instruction in mathematical language and vocabulary.

- Assistive Technology and Accommodations:

  o Examine the role of assistive technology tools in supporting dyslexic learners' academic success.

  o Discuss the use of speech-to-text software, text-to-speech tools, and word prediction software to address writing and reading challenges.

oHighlight the importance of implementing appropriate accommodations, such as extended time for assignments, alternative assessment formats, and preferential seating.

Throughout this section, we emphasise the need for ongoing assessment, progress monitoring, and data-driven instruction to ensure that interventions are effective and responsive to learners' evolving needs. Collaborative partnerships with specialists, support services, and parents play a crucial role in implementing targeted interventions, providing tailored support, and fostering a comprehensive approach to academic success for dyslexic learners.

By employing these strategies and interventions, educators can create inclusive learning environments that empower dyslexic learners to reach their full potential academically. By recognising and building on their strengths, providing targeted support, and implementing evidence-based practices, we can foster the academic growth and achievement of dyslexic learners.

Fostering Social-Emotional Well-Being

In this section, we delve into strategies and practices aimed at fostering the social-emotional well-being of dyslexic learners. Recognising that dyslexia can have a significant impact on learners' self-esteem, confidence, and overall emotional well-being, we explore approaches that nurture positive self-perception, resilience, and a sense of belonging.

- Creating a Dyslexia-Friendly Classroom:
    - oDiscuss the importance of creating a supportive and inclusive learning environment that celebrates neurodiversity.
    - oExplore strategies for setting clear expectations, establishing routines, and providing a safe space for open communication.
    - oHighlight the significance of promoting a growth mindset and re-framing challenges as opportunities for growth and learning.

◎ Building Self-esteem and Self-awareness:

    o Examine approaches for fostering positive self-esteem and self-image in dyslexic learners.

    o Discuss the importance of helping learners recognise their strengths, talents, and unique abilities.

    o Highlight the role of self-reflection, self-advocacy, and self-acceptance in building self-awareness and confidence.

◎ Addressing Anxiety and Stress:

    o Explore strategies for helping dyslexic learners manage anxiety and stress related to academic tasks and social situations.

    o Discuss the importance of providing a supportive and calm learning environment, establishing stress-reduction techniques, and teaching coping strategies.

    o Highlight the role of mindfulness, relaxation exercises, and effective time management in alleviating anxiety.

◎ Promoting Resilience and Growth Mindset:

    o Examine approaches for fostering resilience and a growth mindset in dyslexic learners.

    o Discuss the importance of helping learners develop a positive attitude towards challenges and setbacks.

    o Highlight the role of goal setting, perseverance, and celebrating successes in cultivating resilience and a belief in one's abilities.

◎ Cultivating Positive Relationships and Empathy:

    o Explore strategies for fostering positive relationships among dyslexic learners and their peers.

    o Discuss the importance of promoting empathy, understanding, and inclusivity within the classroom.

    o Highlight the role of cooperative learning, peer support, and inclusive social activities in building a sense of community.

◎ Collaborating with Supportive Professionals and Parents:
  o Discuss the significance of collaboration with educational psychologists, counsellors, and other professionals to provide comprehensive support.
  o Explore strategies for effective communication and collaboration with parents, fostering a partnership that promotes the well-being of dyslexic learners.
  o Highlight the importance of shared goals, information sharing, and regular updates to ensure a holistic approach to supporting learners.

Throughout this section, we emphasise the need for educators to be sensitive, compassionate, and understanding in their interactions with dyslexic learners. By creating a nurturing environment, addressing anxiety, promoting resilience, and fostering positive relationships, we can support the social-emotional well-being of dyslexic learners, empowering them to navigate challenges, build confidence, and thrive in all aspects of their lives.

Collaboration and Support

In this section, we explore the importance of collaboration and support in effectively meeting the needs of dyslexic learners. Recognising that dyslexia support requires a multi-faceted approach, we delve into the roles and contributions of various specialists, support services, and collaborative partnerships.
◎ Collaborating with Educational Psychologists:
  o Discuss the role of educational psychologists in assessing and diagnosing dyslexia.
  o Explore the importance of collaboration with educational psychologists in understanding learners' strengths, challenges, and individualised needs.
  o Highlight the significance of incorporating assessment data and recommendations into instructional planning and interventions.

◎   Partnering with Speech and Language Therapists:

  o Discuss the role of speech and language therapists in addressing communication difficulties and language-based challenges.

  o Explore the collaborative approach between educators and speech and language therapists to support language development, phonological awareness, and expressive skills.

  o Highlight the significance of implementing recommended strategies and incorporating speech and language therapy goals into classroom practices.

◎   Engaging with Occupational Therapists:

  o Discuss the role of occupational therapists in addressing fine motor skills, visual-motor integration, and sensory processing challenges.

  o Explore collaborative efforts between educators and occupational therapists to promote handwriting skills, organisation, and self-regulation.

  o Highlight the importance of incorporating occupational therapy recommendations into classroom routines and providing accommodations as needed.

◎   Collaborating with Learning Support Teams:

  o Discuss the role of learning support teams in providing additional support and resources for learners with diverse needs.

  o Explore the collaborative efforts between educators, learning support teams, and specialists to develop individualised education plans (IEPs) and support students' unique requirements.

  o Highlight the significance of regular communication, data sharing, and joint decision-making to ensure a comprehensive and cohesive approach to support.

◎   Partnering with Inclusion Coordinators:

  o Discuss the role of inclusion coordinators in promoting

inclusive practices and supporting the needs of dyslexic learners within the broader school context.

- o Explore collaborative partnerships between educators and inclusion coordinators in developing and implementing school-wide policies, professional development programs, and inclusive strategies.
- o Highlight the importance of fostering a whole-school approach to dyslexia support through collaboration and coordination.

⊚ Leveraging Community and Parent Support:
- o Discuss the significance of engaging parents as partners in supporting dyslexic learners.
- o Explore strategies for effective communication, sharing resources, and involving parents in their child's educational journey.
- o Highlight the role of community support groups, advocacy organisations, and online forums in providing additional resources and networks for educators and parents.

Throughout this section, we emphasise the power of collaboration and the importance of building strong partnerships to meet the diverse needs of dyslexic learners. By working together with specialists, support services, inclusion coordinators, and parents, educators can create a cohesive support system that enhances the academic, social-emotional, and overall well-being of dyslexic learners. By valuing the expertise and contributions of each collaborator, we can foster a holistic and inclusive approach to dyslexia support.

Empowering Dyslexic Learners

In this section, we focus on empowering dyslexic learners to take an active role in their own learning, develop self-advocacy skills, and build upon their strengths. By fostering a sense of agency and providing personalised support, we can empower dyslexic learners to navigate challenges, set goals, and achieve success.

- ◎ Personalised Support Plans:
  - o Discuss the importance of developing individualised support plans that address the unique needs and strengths of dyslexic learners.
  - o Explore the collaborative process between educators, specialists, and learners in identifying goals, accommodations, and strategies.
  - o Highlight the significance of regularly reviewing and updating the support plans based on learners' progress and evolving needs.

- ◎ Goal-Setting and Meta-cognitive Strategies:
  - o Discuss the value of goal-setting in fostering motivation, self-awareness, and a sense of purpose in dyslexic learners.
  - o Explore strategies for setting realistic, attainable goals that focus on both academic and personal growth.
  - o Highlight the importance of meta-cognitive strategies, such as self-reflection, self-monitoring, and self-regulation, in promoting independent learning.

- ◎ Executive Function Skills:
  - o Discuss the role of executive function skills, such as organisation, time management, and task prioritisation, in supporting dyslexic learners.
  - o Explore strategies for developing and strengthening executive function skills, both within the classroom and through explicit instruction.
  - o Highlight the importance of providing visual supports, checklists, and routines to help dyslexic learners manage their time and resources effectively.

- ◎ Assistive Technology Tools:
  - o Examine the role of assistive technology tools in supporting dyslexic learners' independence and access to information.
  - o Discuss the use of text-to-speech software, speech-to-text

tools, graphic organisers, and digital note-taking apps.

- oHighlight the importance of providing instruction and support in using assistive technology tools to enhance productivity and overcome specific challenges.

- ⊚ Strengths-Based Approach:
    - oDiscuss the significance of recognising and building upon the strengths and talents of dyslexic learners.
    - oExplore strategies for incorporating project-based learning, creative activities, and problem-solving tasks that tap into their strengths.
    - oHighlight the importance of celebrating successes, fostering a growth mindset, and promoting a positive self-image.

- ⊚ Transition Planning:
    - oDiscuss the importance of supporting dyslexic learners during transitions, such as moving between grade levels or transitioning to higher education or the workforce.
    - oExplore strategies for facilitating smooth transitions, including providing orientation, self-advocacy training, and mentorship opportunities.
    - oHighlight the significance of developing self-advocacy skills to empower dyslexic learners in advocating for their needs and accommodations.
- o

Throughout this section, we emphasise the need to foster a supportive and inclusive learning environment that nurtures dyslexic learners' strengths, bolsters their confidence, and promotes self-determination. By empowering dyslexic learners with personalised support, goal-setting strategies, executive function skills, and assistive technology tools, we equip them with the necessary tools and mindset to overcome challenges, embrace their unique abilities, and succeed academically and beyond.

Looking Ahead

In this final section, we reflect on the evolving landscape of dyslexia support and explore potential future directions in research, policies, and practices. As we conclude this book, we recognise that the journey of supporting dyslexic learners is ongoing, and there are opportunities for growth and improvement.

- ◉ Advancements in Research:
  - o Discuss the importance of ongoing research in deepening our understanding of dyslexia and informing evidence-based practices.
  - o Explore emerging research findings and their implications for dyslexia support.
  - o Highlight the significance of staying updated with current research to enhance instructional approaches and interventions,

- ◉ Policy and Advocacy:
  - o Discuss the role of policies and legislation in promoting inclusive education and supporting the needs of dyslexic learners.
  - o Explore the potential for policy changes and advocacy efforts to improve access to resources, accommodations, and support services.
  - o Highlight the importance of advocating for dyslexia awareness and inclusion at local, national, and international levels.

- ◉ Professional Development:
  - o Emphasise the ongoing need for professional development to equip educators with the knowledge and skills to support dyslexic learners effectively.
  - o Discuss the importance of professional learning communities, conferences, workshops, and online resources in enhancing educators' capacity to meet learners' needs.
  - o Highlight the significance of continuous growth and collaboration among educators and specialists to stay informed about best practices.

- ◎ Collaboration and Partnerships:
  - oEmphasise the value of collaboration among educators, specialists, parents, and support services in providing comprehensive support to dyslexic learners.
  - oDiscuss the potential for strengthening collaboration through inter-professional partnerships, joint professional development, and knowledge sharing platforms.
  - oHighlight the importance of fostering a collaborative culture that embraces diverse perspectives and expertise.

- ◎ Inclusive Practices:
  - oDiscuss the potential for expanding inclusive practices beyond dyslexia to support learners with a range of learning differences.
  - oExplore the use of Universal Design for Learning (UDL) principles to create inclusive and accessible learning environments.
  - oHighlight the importance of embracing neurodiversity and creating inclusive education systems that value and celebrate individual differences.

As we look ahead, we are hopeful for a future that embraces the strengths, talents, and potential of dyslexic learners. By staying informed, collaborating, advocating, and continuously evolving our practices, we can create inclusive educational environments that empower dyslexic learners to thrive academically, socially, and emotionally. Let us embark on this journey together, supporting dyslexic learners with compassion, knowledge, and unwavering dedication.

Conclusion

In this book, we have explored the multifaceted aspects of supporting dyslexic learners, providing educators with a comprehensive guide to understanding dyslexia, implementing effective strategies, and fostering a supportive learning environment. As we conclude this journey, let us reflect on the key messages and the transformative impact we can have on the lives of dyslexic learners.

Dyslexia is a neurodiverse condition that presents unique challenges in the realm of learning, but it does not define the potential and abilities of individuals. By understanding dyslexia and its characteristics, we can dispel misconceptions and create an inclusive environment that celebrates the strengths and talents of dyslexic learners.

Throughout the book, we have explored a range of strategies and interventions tailored to address the specific needs of dyslexic learners. From differentiated instruction and multi-sensory approaches to the use of assistive technology and accommodations, we have learned how to meet learners at their point of need and promote their academic success.

Furthermore, we have recognised the importance of fostering social-emotional well-being in dyslexic learners. By creating a dyslexia-friendly classroom, building self-esteem, addressing anxiety, and cultivating resilience, we can nurture the holistic development of dyslexic learners and help them thrive in all aspects of their lives.

Collaboration has been a recurring theme, as we have explored the crucial role of specialists, support services, parents, and professionals in providing comprehensive support to dyslexic learners. By fostering collaborative partnerships, we can leverage diverse expertise, share resources, and create a cohesive support system that addresses the unique needs of dyslexic learners.

Looking ahead, we recognise the need for ongoing research, policy changes, professional development, and the expansion of inclusive practices to further enhance dyslexia support. By staying informed, advocating for change, and embracing innovative approaches, we can continually evolve our practices to better meet the needs of dyslexic learners.

As we conclude this book, let us remain committed to the mission of supporting dyslexic learners and creating inclusive educational environments. Every learner deserves the opportunity to thrive and succeed, and by implementing the strategies and approaches presented in this book, we can make a lasting impact on the lives of dyslexic learners.

To all educators, specialists, parents, and professionals dedicated to the well-being and success of dyslexic learners, I extend my deepest gratitude. Together, we can empower dyslexic learners, celebrate their unique abilities, and create a more inclusive and equitable educational landscape. Let us continue to learn, grow, and advocate for the success of dyslexic learners with unwavering dedication and passion.

Printed in Great Britain
by Amazon

30179322R00116